Penguin Education

Penguin Science of Behaviour
General Editor: B. M. Foss

Physiological Psychology
Editor: K. H. Pribram

Vigilance and Attention
A Signal Detection Approach
Jane F. Mackworth

Vigilance and Attention
A Signal Detection Approach

Jane F. Mackworth

Penguin Books

To Karl Pribram, the Frontiersman

Penguin Books Ltd., Harmondsworth,
Middlesex, England
Penguin Books Inc., 7110 Ambassador Road,
Baltimore, Md. 21207, U.S.A.
Penguin Books Australia Ltd.,
Ringwood, Victoria, Australia

First published 1970
Copyright © Jane F. Mackworth, 1970

Printed in the United States of America by
Universal Litho.
Set in Monotype Times

Penguin Science of Behaviour

This book is one of an ambitious project, the *Penguin Science of Behaviour*, which covers a very wide range of psychological inquiry. Many of the short 'unit' texts are on central teaching topics, while others deal with present theoretical and empirical work which the Editors consider to be important new contributions to psychology. We have kept in mind both the teaching divisions of psychology and also the needs of psychologists at work. For readers working with children, for example, some of the units in the field of Developmental Psychology deal with psychological techniques in testing children, other units deal with work on cognitive growth. For academic psychologists, there are units in well-established areas such as Learning and Perception, but also units which do not fall neatly under any one heading, or which are thought of as 'applied', but which nevertheless are highly relevant to psychology as a whole.

The project is published in short units for two main reasons. Firstly, a large range of short texts at inexpensive prices gives the teacher a flexibility in planning his course and recommending texts for it. Secondly, the pace at which important new work is published requires the project to be adaptable. Our plan allows a unit to be revised or a fresh unit to be added with maximum speed and minimal cost to the reader.

Above all, for students, the different viewpoints of many authors, sometimes overlapping, sometimes in contradiction, and the range of topics Editors have selected will reveal the complexity and diversity which exist beyond the necessarily conventional headings of an introductory course.

B.M.F.

Contents

Editorial Foreword

Norman Mackworth is currently a colleague here at Stanford, so I have asked him to contribute his experience and wisdom to editing these reviews. It is only fitting therefore that we introduce this second volume on vigilance together. [KHP]

Vigilance has grown twenty-one years since the first publication on this topic. Within this brief historical perspective, the vigilance story illustrates, in the happiest possible manner, a general lesson or unwritten commandment for all investigators: love thy scientific neighbour; his ideas may soon become your own. Basic to behaviour is this problem of the nature of attention – and general implications for psychology are equally clear. Many of the best answers are coming from the most venturesome spirits who are daring to cross some well-established frontiers in order to create new roads linking isolated disciplines.

Let us take one example: most of the first volume by Jane Mackworth on *Vigilance and Habituation* emphasized the great strengthening of the evidence found when the cross-beams from neurophysiology were added to those available from experimental psychology. The present volume on *Vigilance and Attention* hammers home this same interdisciplinary message. But here the evidence comes from a quite different scientific world – the mathematical psychology of now-you-see-it-and-now-you-don't, the discipline that is more formally known as Signal Detection Theory.

One of the quietest revolutions of our time took place when electronic engineers and mathematicians (such as Tanner and Swets) dared to question some century-old ideas about the nature of human thresholds for sensory inputs. They emphasized, more clearly than ever before, that far more was involved than simply the sensitivity of the human observer in discriminating between the potential signals. In fact, they dealt with the decision processes in perception. They established that whether or not a given physical stimulus is accepted as a signal depends partly upon the criterion adopted by the human observer. His specific choices on signal versus no-signal are based on a more general judgment. Indeed, he always strikes a balance between the *costs* expected from any missed signal, and those resulting from a false alarm. Costly missed signals make him accept more signals; costly false alarms make him accept fewer signals. Therefore quite different decisions may follow exactly the same stimulus events, even if the sensitivity remains unchanged. The battle still rages around the extent to which the undoubted increase in missed signals, found with prolonged attention over time, is due solely to a more exacting criterion with the passage of time, or is due also to changes in observing responses and in sensitivity. Such reduced sensitivity may appear in visual tasks with very rapid or continuous event rates, and in later sessions with various tasks.

Finally, in this book, the neurophysiological and signal detection theories are expertly combined. For instance, Jane Mackworth has emphasized that the apparently straight-forward changes in criterion level with time on task may in fact also be arising from neurophysiological effects other than those involved in changing expectancies about the likelihood of there being a signal at the moment of decision. These apparently psychological changes in the criterion may in fact arise from habituation of the neural responses evoked by the signal itself and by the non-signal events. Costs of a different kind enter here, since habituation increases the difficulty of attending to the situation, both overtly and psychologically. There are therefore always *two* kinds of yes-no choices; the first decision is whether or not to observe the display at all before any signal versus no-signal choice can be made. This initial observing response could be habituating out, with performance effects very similar to those that would arise from an altered criterion.

The volume is rich in such insights derived from the vast quantities of data that have been accumulated over the past decades. The reader will be amply rewarded for his vigilance and attention to this uncommon review.

K.H.P.

N. M.

1 Introduction

The concept of attention has recently returned to favour in psychological and physiological research. It is acquiring not only a qualitative but even a quantitative aspect, with the borrowing of the idea of capacity from information theory, biology and physics. The animal or human is more than a stimulus–response machine; he actively searches for and selects those stimuli that are important to him, and he increases their impact by a whole range of physiological and psychological processes. At the same time, the effect of stimuli judged to be unimportant is inhibited.

However, it remains hard to define attention without circularity. In general terms, it can be considered as a mental faculty that *selects* one or more external stimuli or internal mental events or traces. It is as basic to the human psychological experiment as gravity is to the universe, and as often forgotten as gravity used to be. Psychological studies on the human nearly always begin with directing the subject's attention towards the material that is the basis of the experiment, asking the subject to learn this, discriminate that, or rank order those stimuli, and so on. In most experiments the nature of the task is such that the subject finds it interesting, and has no difficulty in maintaining the necessary attention. Consequently, failures of attention need not be taken into account. In the vigilance task, however, it is probable that the important variable is just this faculty of attention.

Hebb has commented on the 'doubled train of thought' that enables the mind to view itself, and he pointed out that there is no need to call this activity introspection. 'It is quite respectable for an objective psychologist to have imagery and report it; his virginity is not thereby brought into question' (Hebb, 1969, p. 56). He might have added that it is perhaps time for this pristine innocence to be fertilized by the physiologist. Such a marriage has already produced much valuable data on the psychological and physiological concomitants of the elusive process of attention.

In its simplest form, the process of attention can be seen in the act of looking towards one stimulus; this act also involves looking away from another. The normal human will almost always look towards the source of an external stimulus which interests him. N. H. Mackworth and Morandi (1967) have shown that subjects looking at pictures rest their gaze most frequently on areas judged to be highly informative, and reject considerable areas of such pictures without ever looking directly at these uninformative areas. The fact that the gaze is resting directly on an item does not, however, mean that the subject is paying attention to it, nor that he will notice and report the item, even if he is searching for it (Mackworth and Mackworth, 1958b). The observing response includes physiological changes and is only the outward manifestation of an internal process. As Trabasso and Bower (1968) point out in their summary of the history of the concept of attention, attempts to separate attention into peripheral or central processes are useless. The observing response has been brought into the theoretical discussions of vigilance, but its meaning must probably be enlarged so that it becomes simply the paying of attention to a stimulus. It is possible that attention can vary in two dimensions: it can be directed to one stimulus source (or to a thought) or to another, or it can be divided between two dimensions of the task. It is also possible that it can vary in total capacity in a vertical fashion, there being more available capacity when the organism is aroused than when it is drowsy.

There are two main aspects of the concept of attention, relating to the qualities of the *object* of attention and to the state of the *organism* that is directing his attention. Whether or not an individual directs attention towards a particular stimulus depends on the interaction between these two aspects. The stimulus has certain intrinsic qualities, and certain qualities which are invested in it, as it were, by the past history of the organism. Any unfamiliar, novel, unusually intense or unexpected stimulus will tend to produce the orienting response, which involves a whole chain of psychological and physiological activities devoted to the identification of the stimulus. The reasons why attention continues to be paid to an identified stimulus or series of stimuli are manifold. Here enter such factors as informativeness, relevance, interest, emotional content and so on. In this book we are more concerned with the opposite question. Why does an observer become less efficient in performance as he continues to work at a monotonous task?

The *vigilance task* was originally devised by N. H. Mackworth (1950). It consisted in a highly monotonous task in which the chief difficulty was the temporal irregularity of the signal. One such task was the Clock Test. Here the subject sat alone in a cubicle for two hours, watching a clock hand jerking round in regular jumps, one jump a second, one hundred jumps per revolution. The signal was a jump of twice the usual distance. The interval between successive signals varied from 0·75–10 minutes, twelve signals being presented each half-hour. There was thus a signal to non-signal event ratio of 1–150. It was found that the mean proportion of signals detected fell from 85 per cent in the first half hour to about 73 per cent in the second and subsequent half-hours. This fall in detections constituted the original 'vigilance decrement', and the problem was to determine the reason for it.

The vigilance decrement has been found in a wide range of tasks (see Appendix). It has been found that in addition to the reduction in detection probability, there is often a reduction in false alarms, suggesting that the subject is less inclined to make a positive response, right or wrong. When the signal is easily seen, then there is usually a decrease in the speed of response during the session.

Decrements in speed and accuracy of response have also

been found in more active tasks, such as tracking tasks, or continuous threshold measurements. Such tasks also require continuous attention to a highly monotonous and repetitive display, with some temporal uncertainty. Therefore it would appear that the very low probability that an event will be a signal, as found in a vigilance task, is not the only cause of the decrement in performance.

Several theoretical explanations of the decrement have been advanced. Each emphasizes some aspects of the task, and none includes all the facts. The aim of this book (see also J. F. Mackworth, 1969) is to show how they may be fitted together to produce a more coherent whole. Such explanations or theories fall into two classes, those theories primarily physiological and those primarily psychological. Which is more basic is a question equivalent to the primacy of the chicken or the egg. It is hoped that these books will help to bring the two classes together.

The outline of the viewpoint adopted here is that repetition and monotony produce habituation of physiological responses, particularly neural ones, and that as a result of such habituation it becomes increasingly difficult for the subject to continue to pay attention to the task. His attention will fluctuate, and perhaps also his level of arousal will be reduced, so that he becomes drowsy. During such periods when he is no longer paying active attention to the display, he will cease to make responses of any kind, right or wrong, or he will react more slowly to obvious changes that do attract his attention (see Broadbent, 1958). Such fluctuations in the level of responsiveness to a particular stimulus would appear to be quite different from alternation of attention between two sources (Broadbent and Gregory, 1963a).

Neurophysiological theories of the decrement include neural *inhibition*, reductions in the level of *arousal*, and changes in the amplitude and pattern of the *evoked potential*, the neurological response to the repetitive stimulus that constitutes the background events of the task. These have been fully dealt with elsewhere (J. F. Mackworth, 1969). There it was suggested that *habituation of the neural potentials* (evoked by the repetitive background events of the task, or by the slight change in these events which constitutes the signal to be detected), may result in a decrease in both correct and incorrect positive responses. This change thus appears as an apparent increase in the strictness of the criterion (see chapter 2). This decrease may, however, be due simply to the fact that fewer neural events, both signal and non-signal, reach the criterial level after habituation has occurred. The neural 'arousal response' usually consists in a decrease in the amplitude of the neural 'noise' as the background rhythms are suppressed. At the beginning of a task such arousal responses may be prolonged, but they will gradually become shorter, and finally may disappear. The occurrence of a signal may perhaps briefly reinstate such an arousal response. The effect of this initial decrease in the background neural noise may be to lower the threshold for the signal, and habituation of the arousal responses may result in an increase in threshold. Such changes may be most marked in tasks with continuous or very rapid event rates, in which each individual event may not evoke a separate neural potential change. Habituation of other aspects of the orienting response may also result in increased thresholds (see J. F. Mackworth, 1969). Habituation of the evoked response to the background events may on the other hand lower the threshold for small changes in these events. This will counteract the decreased sensitivity due to reduction in arousal discussed above, especially in early sessions with fairly slow discrete background events.

The discussion of the *observing responses* (chapter 4) links the psychological and physiological aspects. The subject may choose whether or not to pay attention to the display. Due perhaps to habituation, it becomes increasingly difficult for him to pay continuous attention, so he may limit his observing responses to those times when he thinks a signal is most likely. This is the *expectancy aspect* (chapter 5). Such intermittent attention may help to counteract habituation. As a result of changes in expectancy, the subject may change his criterial level, and give fewer positive responses, either right or wrong. This change may be most marked in the first session.

Aspects of the vigilance task that are particularly related to habituation and the level of arousal are dealt with elsewhere (J. F. Mackworth, 1969). There evidence has been considered in detail relating to individual variation, and to the effects of such external factors as drugs. The main conclusions were:

1. Physiological indices of arousal change during a vigilance task, but there is little evidence that these changes are directly related to the decrement in performance. Individuals vary in their patterns of physiological responses, and also there is little relationship between performance on two different kinds of vigilance task. Adequate studies of all physiological indices and performance measures for each individual are rare.

2. The few experiments relating vigilance performance to evoked potentials have suggested a direct relationship, but the nature of this relationship is as yet obscure. There may be a decrease in the positive amplitude of the visual evoked potential (Haider *et al.*, 1964), or an increase in the late negative wave in an auditory task (Wilkinson *et al.*, 1966).

3. The main positive finding with regard to individual differences was that introverts are likely to do better than extraverts. The quality of 'achievement through independence' (Halcomb and Kirk, 1965) has also been found to be related to vigilance performance.

4. Loss of sleep may increase the rate of decrement, especially when the task is familiar. Noise may also increase the rate of decrement, and reduce the number of doubtful decisions (Broadbent and Gregory, 1965). Noise may, however, counteract the effects of sleep loss, indicating that these two stresses act on different mechanisms.

5. Environmental variety, such as music or jokes, may reduce the decrement.

6. There appears to be an optimal environmental temperature. Cold may reduce performance throughout, while heat may increase the rate of decrement.

7. Stimulants prevent the decrement in detections, while

depressant drugs increase it. The effect of these drugs on false alarms is, however, different from their effect on detections. While the normal subject usually shows a decrease in both detections and false alarms during an early session, stimulants maintain the detections, while the false alarms may decrease as usual. Thus there may be a tendency for sensitivity (d', see chapter 2), to be higher at the end of the drug session as compared with the control session. Similarly, depressants may increase the false alarm rate, or at least maintain it, while increasing the decrement in detections. It would therefore appear that the normal changes in detections and false alarms are not necessarily both due to the same cause. A similar conclusion is drawn from the differential effect of repeated sessions on detections and false alarms (see chapter 7). These and other findings have contributed to the suggestion that there may be two neural processes at work in the vigilance task, (a) habituation of the evoked potential, and (b) habituation of the arousal response.

It is hoped that bringing the data together in this way may lead to a more detailed testing of the basic psychophysiological aspects of a task that seems particularly well adapted for such a study. Psychologists tend to overload their subjects, finding upper limits of behaviour, while physiologists tend to use stimuli of little relevance to the subject. The vigilance task, while originally designed for stimulating practical monitoring, is situated neatly in the middle of these two extremes of stimulation.

A further possible reunion may be briefly discussed at this point. Western science has tended to oversimplify, although every reduction to 'nothing but' has been followed by a new expansion. The stimulus–response machine is now being expanded to allow for attention and other annoying variables that refuse to be permanently eliminated. Eastern science has also attempted to reduce the unending range of phenomena to categories; many thousands of years ago the Indian teachers recognized at least five basic processes occurring between the object and its apprehension by the conscious mind. These categories are very relevant to our subject of vigilance and attention, so a brief summary might be of interest. The teachings of Yoga have been summarized by Taimni (1965, p.269). He described these five stages: (1) the object, (2) the sense organs, (3) sensations, (4) the mind and (5) perception. The joining of the mind (attention) to sensations results in perception. As Western psychology might say, the joining of sensations to the established model or memory trace results in classification.

Yoga recognizes three levels of ordinary consciousness: awake, asleep and dreamless sleep; it is clear that these correspond to the concept of different levels of arousal. It would seem that a description of the processes being examined in the vigilance task can be made very well in these terms. The whole system is a two-way process. Energy flows from the stimulus to the organism, and energy also flows from the aroused mind to direct and activate the sense organs, which thus select and receive extra energy from the selected stimulus. At the same time, the mind considers the incoming stream of information, and constructs perceptions or models that indicate the probability that an event will be a signal. As a result of the very low probability of a signal, the two-way stream of energy is damped down, attention becomes intermittent, and the level of awareness is reduced.

The experienced lecturer or teacher is only too well aware of the difficulty his audience may find in paying attention to a monotonous stimulus, whether it be the voice of the speaker or a stream of slides. By the addition of jokes, unexpected and startling pictures, and, where appropriate, the raising of the level of arousal by emotional remarks, such an experienced speaker will seek to maintain the interest of his audience. Gestures, changes in the loudness or pitch of his voice, provocative statements, anything that interferes with the monotony will help. We are faced with vigilance tasks for a greater part of the day than we realize. Driving is one example. Operating a calculating machine, typing, inspecting endless parts for a flaw, even listening to an unending stream of patients; all these and many other familiar and monotonous tasks may lead to devasting consequences when an error or failure to catch the small but vital symptom may be disastrous. Kamiya (1969) has shown that subjects can learn to control their alpha rhythm, and to be aware of its presence. Moreover, such alpha control also affects the amplitude of the evoked potential (Spilker *et al.*, 1969). It is not yet clear what is the relation between alpha and alertness, but if we could learn to be aware of our own inner states in this way, and adjust them as required, this might be one of the most valuable lessons that we could ever learn. We could then do without the drugs that we now take to keep us alert.

2 Decision Theory in Relation to Vigilance

Until fairly recently it has been assumed that the probability that an observer will report a signal depends solely on his ability to detect the signal. False alarms, usually very few in number, were regarded as unimportant. It has, however, been demonstrated in psychophysical experiments that the decision of an observer to give a response to an observation depends not only on the physical nature of the stimulus reaching his senses, but also on his *criterion*. He can decide to operate with a very lax criterion, in which case he will detect more signals, but also give more false alarms, or he can employ a stricter criterion, giving fewer correct positive responses, and fewer false alarms. The level at which he sets his criterion depends on the relative costs and rewards of the various possible outcomes. There are at least four possible outcomes: there may or may not have been a signal present at a particular time, and the observer may or may not decide to make a response. A brief popular account of decision theory was presented by Edwards *et al.* (1965). A more detailed account can be found in Green and Swets (1966).

It has been suggested by Jerison and Pickett (1963), following Holland (1957, 1963), that there are in fact two successive processes of decision in a vigilance task. Firstly, there is the decision to observe the task, and secondly, there is the decision whether or not to make a response on the basis of that observation. Signal detection theory applies mainly to the second of the two processes, but it will be discussed first, because much of Jerison's argument rests upon the anomalies found in the application of signal detection theory to vigilance data.

Signal Detection Theory in Vigilance

Signal detection theory (SDT) is based on the assumption that there is no such thing as a threshold for detection of signals by an observer. It assumes that there is an overlap between the distributions of noise alone, and signal plus noise, so that any particular observation might have come from either distribution. It is then the task of the observer to decide whether or not he will accept this event as a signal. This decision is made on the basis of the probability that the event is a signal and the values attached by the observer to the decisions that he could make. A simple example of this kind of decision is to be found in the case of the man who sees a pink elephant. He sees this elephant very clearly, but he is aware that it is extremely improbable that there would really be such an event in the external world, and therefore he decides that the event is a consequence of the internal 'noise' arising from a disordered central nervous system. Nevertheless, there is a finite probability that this is a real external event, and automatic rejection of the highly unlikely may lead to trouble if, in fact, there is a pink elephant present.

Green and Swets (1966) have described signal detection theory with great clarity, and therefore it is unnecessary to do more than outline the relevant aspects here. There are many assumptions involved in the calculation of statistics relating to the theory. It is doubtful whether these assumptions can be met in the vigilance situation. Nevertheless, the theory offers a first step towards the essential process of dividing the *sensitivity* of the observer from his *criterion*. The basic essential in determining these aspects of performance is the observation interval. It is necessary to know how often the observer makes a decision. In the standard SDT experiment, the observation intervals are clearly marked. In a vigilance experiment they may be marked, when the events are discrete, or there may be an unchanging or continuous background from which the signal must be distinguished. In such a case, certain arbitrary assumptions must be made about the observation interval.

Two measures are essential for determining SDT statistics of *sensitivity* (*detectability*) and *criterion*. These two measures are the proportion of signals that receive a positive response and the proportion of non-signal events which receive a positive response. In vigilance experiments these are usually measured as the percentage of correct detections and the percentage of false alarms. In an SDT experiment there are two main ways of determining the *detectability* of the signal for the observer. One is the *forced-choice method* and the other is the ROC curve (or *yes–no method*). In the *forced-choice method* an observer is presented with two or more observation intervals and asked to say which of them contained the signal. Such a method is independent of the criterion of the observer. All his responses are either correct or false positives. In the *yes–no method* the aim is to construct a Receiver Operating Characteristic curve (ROC). This can be done either by asking the observer to maintain a different criterion in separate sessions, or by asking him to rate his responses according to several criteria, such as 'sure', 'almost sure' down to 'sure no'. By this means several points are obtained which are assumed to represent the same detectability with different criteria. Then a plot of the proportion of correct detections against the proportion of non-signal events that received a positive answer gives the ROC curve. The area under this curve represents the *detectability* of the signal (see Figure 1). This method has the great advantage that it is independent of any assumptions made about the distributions of the noise or signal plus noise. The *criterial level* is measured by the statistic *beta* (β), which is the slope of the ROC curve at the operating point.

The basic assumption of signal detection theory that there is no threshold leads to the further assumption that false positive responses are not guesses but are responses to an event that has a finite probability of being a signal. Whether or not this event receives a positive response depends on the criterion of the subject. With a more lax criterion he will give more positive responses, some of which will be correct and others which will be incorrect. Hence as his criterion becomes more lax, he will detect more signals and he will give more

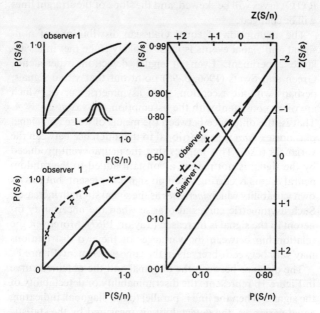

Figure 1 Empirical data from an auditory signal detection task. P(S/s) is the probability of a correct response, given that a signal occurred (correct detections). P(S/n) is the probability of a positive response when no signal was present (false alarm probability). The theoretical curves are based on the assumptions of normal probability distributions of equal and unequal variances respectively. The inserts represent the probability distributions underlying the curves. The curve for observer 2 is based on the assumption that $\triangle m / \triangle \sigma = 4$ (Green and Swets, 1966)

false alarms. Figure 1 illustrates R O C curves obtained when the distributions of noise and signal plus noise are normal probability distributions. Under such circumstances the R O C curves become straight lines when plotted on linear normal-deviate scales. If the distributions are of equal variance, then the ROC curves will be parallel to the positive diagonal. If the distributions are not of equal variance, then the ROC curves will be skewed, and the slope of the straight lines will be changed.

The assumption of equal Gaussian distributions of non-signal and signal events is most unlikely to be met in a vigilance experiment. Even in signal detection experiments, Green and Swets (1966, p. 98) point out that visual signals, perhaps without exception, yield asymmetric curves, which are often consistent with the assumption that $\Delta m / \Delta \sigma = 4$. That is, the difference between the means of noise and signal plus noise (Δm) is proportional to the difference between the variances ($\Delta \sigma$). This implies that the neural event produced by the signal is not merely a constant added to the random neural events occurring when no signal is present, but has its own variability which *increases* as the signal strength increases. Such asymmetric curves also arise when the uncertainty inherent in the signal is increased (Taylor, 1967). Moreover, the relationship between the variances of the two distributions may vary between observers in the same experiment (Figure 1).

The distance between the diagonal and the obtained curve in Figure 1b represents the discriminability or detectability of the signal. When the line is parallel to the diagonal, indicating equal variances, the detectability is measured by the statistic d'. The slope of the ROC curve at the operating point gives the criterial level at that point and is known as *beta* (β). Values for d' and *beta*, under the assumption of equal Gaussian variances, can be obtained from tables prepared for this purpose (Swets, 1964; P. R. Freeman, 1964). Taylor (1967) has pointed out that if these tables are used for the determination of detectability and criterial values when unequal variances are present, the estimated values for d' and *beta* will be too high. Changes in d' will probably represent real changes in detectability, provided that the criterial level is not changed by the experimental procedures. Changes in *beta* are more dubious.

Green and Swets further pointed out (1966, p. 227) that if

the standard deviation of the internal noise is related to the mean value of the pedestal or non-signal event to which the signal is added, then Weber's Law can be predicted. This law states that the intensity of a stimulus change that can just be detected is a constant fraction of the background intensity. In other words, as the background or non-signal events in a vigilance task increase in intensity, the increment or change in these events that can just be detected as a signal increases. Alternatively, the sensitivity for a particular increment is reduced as the background intensity is increased. The converse is also true. A slightly different explanation for Weber's Law in signal detection theory terms has been advanced by M. Treisman (1964, 1966). He has shown theoretically and by simulation that at very low intensities the uncorrelated physical noise will have a greater effect, leading to the square root law, but as the background intensities increase, the correlated sensory noise will increase in relative importance, so that Weber's Law comes into effect.

As the background or non-signal events of a vigilance task increase in intensity, Weber's Law predicts that the small change in an event that constitutes a signal will become less discriminable. The converse is also true. Thus if the neural responses to the repetitive events habituate so that the amplitude of the evoked potential is reduced, sensitivity to the signal may actually *increase*. If, on the other hand, the main change is an increase in amplitude, as shown by Wilkinson *et al.* (1966), sensitivity to the signal may decrease. Wilkinson *et al.* have suggested that this increase in the late negative evoked potential is related to a decrease in the level of activation. Habituation of the E E G response, the alpha block, may result in an increase in the variance of the neural noise. Occurrence of the sleep patterns, the theta rhythm and spindles, will also increase the variance of the background neural noise. Such a change may result in a decrease in sensitivity to the signal, especially if the background events are not clearly distinguishable from the noise, because they are continuous or very fast.

If the neural response evoked by the background event is decreased in amplitude, as a result of habituation, then if the strength of neural event that is given an overt response is unchanged, the result will be a decrease in both correct detections and false alarms. This will occur because fewer neural events will now reach this criterial level, so that an apparent change in criterion may actually be a result of a constant criterion acting on a decreased strength of neural response.

Temporal uncertainty

Egan *et al.* (1961a) studied the effect of time uncertainty on detection. Most signal detection experiments are carried out under conditions in which the observer knows exactly the interval during which there will or will not be a signal. Egan *et al.* varied the Interval of Time Uncertainty (I T U), defined as the interval during which the signal may have its onset, from 0 to 8 seconds. They found that d' fell by over 0.5 units as the I T U was increased, with most of the fall occurring between 0 and 2 seconds. It may be pointed out that the interval of time uncertainty for a signal in a vigilance task is directly related to the rate of background events. For a given signal rate, the uncertainty of the signal onset increases as the number of events between signals increase.

Egan *et al.* (1961b) extended this work to a situation even more like a vigilance task. Signals were presented against a background of continuous random noise with intersignal intervals varying from 3.5 to 15.5 seconds. Each 'listening period' was two minutes long, with fifteen-second rests between listening periods, indicated by signal lights. Subjects were required to adopt different criteria in different sessions. Responses were plotted according to the time of occurrence, in relation to the signal. It was found that the response rate rose sharply in the first second after a signal and then fell to a very low level by two seconds after the signal. With the more lax criteria, the response level then rose slowly again. The area under the peak of the curve was taken as D, and the area under the curve 3·2 seconds after the signal was taken as O or the operant rate. From these values d' values were obtained. It was shown that log D was directly proportional to log O, and it was justifiable to assume that there was a relationship between detections and false alarms.

The relationship between d' and the energy of the signal was determined in these experiments with free response and also with a fixed interval. It was found that in each case the relationship could be represented by a straight line, but the slope was greater with the fixed interval. Thus the difference between the detectability of the signal with temporal uncertainty and with a fixed interval increased as the signal strength increased. In a vigilance task the signal detectability is usually high in a pretest. Therefore, the effect of temporal uncertainty would be maximal.

The influence of the probability of the signal on the criterion of the subject was demonstrated by Nachmias (1968). Three signal probabilities, 0·25, 0·50 and 0·75, were employed in a signal detection experiment, in which the subjects were fully informed as to the structure of the experiment. It was found that the data could be represented by a single straight line, on double Gaussian coordinates; points obtained with the low signal probability fell at the lower end of the line, and points obtained with the high probability fell at the upper end. Thus, the subjects altered their criterion according to the signal probability, but the detectability of the signal remained unaltered. The lines had a slope of less than one in this visual experiment (see p. 26).

It is therefore reasonable to suppose that subjects working in a vigilance task will adjust their criterion, if they find that the signal probability is less than they have been expecting. Even if they are aware of the signal probability, they can be expected to adopt a different criterion in a pre-test, in which signals are presented very frequently, than in the experimental vigil, in which there is a very low probability of signals. Such changes in *criterion* have been found in many vigilance tasks. The question remains, however, as to whether this is the only change, or whether there may also be changes in the *ability of the subject to detect the signal.*

Vigilance and signal detectability measures

Criterial changes were demonstrated by Broadbent and Gregory (1963b), who employed the rating method in auditory and visual vigilance tasks. The visual task required the detection of a brighter flash on one of three tubes which flashed simultaneously once every 1·4 seconds for 0·3 seconds. Subjects were asked to press one of four buttons every time they suspected that there had been a signal. These buttons were marked with different categories of certainty that there had been a signal. It was found that the ratio of detections to false-positives became less as responses of lower confidence were included. In other words, the subjects could assess accurately the worth of their own judgments. The increase in detection rate was almost always greater than the increase in false positive rates, showing that the less confident judgments were correct more often than chance alone would allow. No consistent change in detections was found during the session, but there was a reduction in false positives for each criterial level. No changes in d' were found during the session, but *beta* was found to increase during the session with the most cautious criterion, though not with the risky criterion.

Broadbent and Gregory (1965) continued this work with the same visual task, with extra variables. Two signal rates were used, a low rate of one signal, in fifteen flashes, (eighty signals in seventy minutes), and a high rate of one signal in five flashes (240 signals in seventy minutes). The flashes were repeated every 3·5 seconds. The signals were presented on the central tube alone or on any of the three tubes. The results showed:

1. The only significant effect on d' was due to conditions. Fewer false alarms were given with the low signal rate than with the high signal rate, resulting in an apparently higher value for d' (see p. 92). The highest value for d' was found on

the second day with the three-channel test; in this condition a higher luminance was employed for the signal.

2. The criterial level as measured by *beta* showed several significant changes during the experiment.

(a) The highest value was found with the low signal rate; subjects gave fewer incorrect 'sure' responses with this condition.

(b) There was also an increase in *beta* on the second day of testing. Such increases are interpreted as an increasing caution in making a response.

(c) There was an interaction between days and periods during a session. While there was a marked increase in *beta* during the session on the first day, on the second this increase was much reduced. In fact, with the low signal rate there was a decrease in *beta* during the second session. These changes were found with the strict criterion. There was no indication of a shift in the more risky criterion (Broadbent and Gregory, 1965).

The data from this experiment have been redrawn on linear normal-deviate scales (Figure 2); with these scales R O C curves appear as straight lines if they are based on normal distributions (see p. 25). It has been described how these lines will be parallel to the main positive diagonal if the distributions of noise and signal plus noise are of equal variance. It can be seen that the curves for the first three periods of the sessions are not parallel to the diagonal, but are parallel to a line calculated on the basis that $\Delta m = 4 \Delta \sigma$. This suggests that the variances of the noise and signal plus noise distributions are unequal. Green and Swets point out (1966, p. 96) that such unequal variances arise when there is uncertainty about some dimension of the signal. In the final quarter of the session, the slope of the R O C curve is parallel to the diagonal. It is possible that by this time subjects had a better idea of the distribution of signals, though in each case signals were presented in a practice period at the same rate as they were given in the main sessions. There is another possible explanation. If there was an increase in the neural noise during the experiment, due to increased amplitude of the background

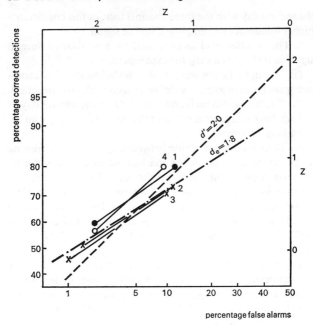

1–4 : periods

theoretical curves

—·—·— $\Delta m = 4 \Delta \sigma$

——— equal variances

Figure 2 Data from a visual vigilance task (Broadbent and Gregory, 1965) replotted on linear normal-deviate scales. Subjects reported 'sure' and 'unsure'. The numbers 1–4 represent successive quarters of a seventy-minute task, with twenty signals in each quarter. Note the apparent change in slope between the third and fourth quarter

neural rhythms, this might result in the variances being less dissimilar then they were at the beginning of the session.

The main conclusion to be drawn from this important work is that great care must be taken in interpreting vigilance data in terms of signal detection theory. Such an analysis is, however, an essential step forward in determining what is really happening.

Green and Swets (1966) pointed out that while visual results usually suggested unequal variances, this was less often found with auditory results. Loeb and Binford (1964) examined changes in an auditory vigilance task. They presented half-second pulses separated by two-second intervals. The signal was a slightly louder pulse, which occurred forty times in eighty minutes. In one session subjects were required to rate their responses with one of three buttons, while in another a simple detection response was required. Detections and false positives decreased during the sessions. The line of best fit to the data from the first and last blocks of trials within each session was $Z(Y/SN) = 1 \cdot 05 \, Z(Y/N) + 2 \cdot 94$. This indicated that the variances of noise and signal plus noise were equal. Two-thirds of the variance in detection probability was predictable from variance in the false positive probability. Two sessions suggested some decrement in d', one session with multiple criterion and one session with the simple vigilance condition. These sessions were the third and fourth in the series. Data from the last multiple criterion session without feedback did suggest a different slope. The authors concluded that the main change in a vigilance task was an increasing *strictness of criterion*, but that in a less closely coupled task, such as a visual one, *decreases in sensitivity* might be more important.

Binford and Loeb (1966), however, did find decrements in d' in later sessions on an auditory task. They found a marked increase in d' between the first and ninth sessions, suggesting that there was some learning, which improved sensitivity. Such an increase in the ability to detect the signal might be obscuring reductions in sensitivity during the early sessions. There was an increase in *beta* between early and late sessions with the multiple criterion, and a significant increase within the early sessions. The authors suggested that the subjects tended to overestimate the probability of a signal at the beginning.

Thus they used a lax criterion, and gave positive responses to more doubtful events than they did late in the tasks, and in later sessions.

The importance of the prior expectancy of the subjects with regard to the temporal distribution of signals has been illustrated by Colquhoun and Baddeley (1967). They examined the effect of training and showed that the criterion of the subject was markedly affected by the signal rate with which he had been trained. In particular, subjects who had been trained with a high signal rate showed a marked increase in *beta* during the session with a low signal rate.

There have been several other experiments which have shown increases in *beta* during a session. Jerison *et al.* (1965) varied the background rate of events (see chapter 4) and found that there were significant increases in *beta* during the sessions with the fast event rate, but no significant changes in d'. Although there were marked differences in detections between the two event rates, and also significant differences in *beta*, there were no differences in d'. Even if false alarms are the same in number in conditions with different event rates, the probability that an event will be a false alarm is, of course, quite different in the two conditions. It is possible that false alarms depend more on the absolute probability of a signal in time than on the relative probability that an event will be a signal.

Levine (1966) varied the costs of missed signals and false alarms in an auditory task. Signals were three different pure tones, presented against a background of noise. No changes in d' were found during the sessions, but *beta* increased in all sessions.

Apparent changes in signal detectability have been consistently found in one task. This is the Continuous Clock, first studied by Baker (1963a and b). In this task the signal is a brief pause in the continuous movement of the second hand of the clock. J. F. Mackworth and Taylor (1963) reported experiments in which d' was estimated under various instructions. It is possible that the reason why changes in d' have been recorded in this task is because it is a visual task that requires continuous attention.

The simplest way to measure *detectability* is the forced-choice method. Here no change in criterion can occur, since the observer has to select the interval in which he considers it most likely that the signal occurred. The area under the yes–no R O C curve equals the percentage of correct responses in a two-alternative forced-choice task (Green and Swets, 1966, p. 48). Thus, the forced-choice method gives a measure of detectability which is independent of the assumptions made about variances. There remains the question as to whether a forced-choice method bears any resemblance to a vigilance task. This question was also examined by the following experiments (J. F. Mackworth and Taylor, 1963).

The clock had a black face, with five-second long white marks at each quarter (see Figure 3). The remaining ten seconds of each quarter were divided into two five-second intervals by a thin white mark. Subjects were told to wait until the hand reached the long white mark before making a response indicating whether there had been a signal in the previous ten seconds. One of the following four sets of instructions was given to each group. There was in fact always one signal in one of the two five-second intervals in each quarter.

1. Forced choice. The subjects were told that there would always be one signal in every quarter minute and they had to make a decision at the end of the ten-second inspection period as to whether the signal was in the first or the second five-second interval, and press one of two labelled response buttons. Six separate groups of seven subjects each worked at this task.

2. The same information was given about the signals, but the subjects were not required to guess if they did not see the signal (unforced choice).

3. The subjects were told that there would be four signals each minute. In this condition they could press both response buttons if they thought there had been a signal in each of the two intervals.

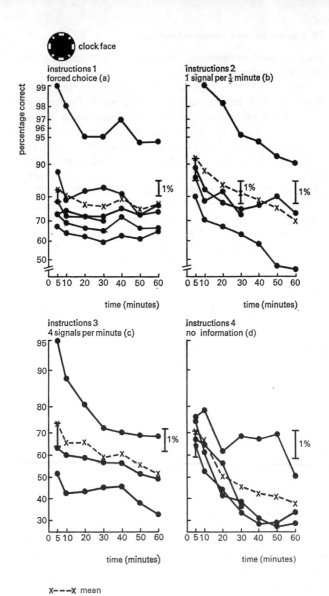

Figure 3a The effect of the instructions upon the percentage of signals correctly detected during an hour's test with the Continuous Clock (J. F. Mackworth and Taylor, 1963)

4. This condition was most like a vigilance task. Subjects were only told that there would never be more than one signal in each quarter minute and as before they had to indicate the interval if they thought they had seen a signal.

The results of these experiments are shown in Figure 3a. The percentage of signals correctly detected during the second ten minutes of the session was less than that detected in the first ten minutes in all the seventeen sessions (each with seven subjects). Significant changes in d' were found during the session. Figure 3 suggests that these changes were related to the initial level, greater decreases in d' being found when the signal was more readily detectable.

Figure 3b shows the logarithm of d' plotted against the

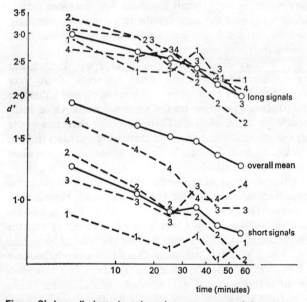

Figure 3b Log d' plotted against the square root of the inspection time for the data shown in Figure 3a. The numbers 1—4 represent the four different instructions (J. F. Mackworth and Taylor, 1963)

square root of time on task. The latter measure was employed because Taylor (1966) had found that performance in a number of tasks involving continuous inspection of an unchanging display showed a linear relation with the square root of time on task (see J. F. Mackworth, 1969).

It was also found that there were many more missed signals in condition 3 than in condition 2. The more detailed information made the subject more likely to guess, even though he knew in both cases that he had a 50 per cent chance of being correct. It can be seen from Figures 3a and 3b that the mean percentage of signals detected was about 80 per cent when the subject was told that there would be a signal every quarter minute, while it fell to 60 per cent when he only knew that there would be four signals a minute. Yet the mean detectability was about the same for the two conditions, resulting from an increased number of false alarms with the more detailed instructions.

In a further experiment the clock face was divided into twelve alternating black and white segments. There were twelve signals per hour on the black segments and either five or 180 signals per hour on the white segments. Once again there were decreases in d'. There were also decreases in the false alarm rate, suggesting that there were increases in *beta*, as found by other authors. More false alarms were given when there were fewer signals.

A further experiment was carried out which showed that these findings were specific for the test used. Signals were presented 180 or thirty times an hour. Two clock tasks were used, the classic Jump Clock test (see chapter 1) and the Continuous Clock. Significant changes in d' during the session were found with the Continuous Clock but not with the Jump Clock (J. F. Mackworth, 1968). The signal rate had little effect on the percentage of signals detected, but more false alarms were given at the slow signal rate, so that the detectability (d') and the criterial level (*beta*) tended to be lower with the slow signal rate. For most groups, especially with the Jump Clock, increases in *beta* during the session were greater with the fast signal rate. With the Jump Clock, d' was significantly higher for the fast signal rate.

It is therefore clear that the Continuous Clock was quite unusual in showing changes in d' during a session. It was thought that this might be due to the fact that the task required a very high rate of observing responses, because the signal could occur at any moment. To test this hypothesis, a task was employed which presented two lights flashing side by side (J. F. Mackworth, 1965c). The signal was a brighter flash of one light. It was found that when the event rate was three flashes per second, there was a significant change in d' during the session, but when the event rate was one flash in 1·2 seconds, no significant change occurred in d'. In both cases there were three signals per minute.

A further experiment was carried out which demonstrated that the *required continuity of observation was the important factor, and not the apparent decision rate*. In the earlier experiment, a decision had to be made every five seconds as to whether there had been a signal in the previous five-second interval. In another experiment (J. F. Mackworth, 1965b), the clock face was blank, and subjects were told to respond immediately after they saw a signal. Values for d' were computed on the basis of six decisions per second, since the signal duration was approximately one-sixth of a second. A further calculation was carried out to see what difference it would make if the values for d' were computed on the previous basis of twelve decisions per minute. It was found that while the assumed decision rate made a large difference in the absolute level of d', it made very little difference in the rate at which d' declined during the session. Moreover, the rate of decline was closely similar to the results found in the original experiment (see Figure 4).

A task that required continuous visual attention was studied by Stern (1966). The subjects were required to watch a steady small point of light and detect occasional movements. Signal rates of one and two per minute were used. Both groups showed a decrement in detections, and an increase in false alarms, indicating a decrease in d', during the session. The group receiving the low signal rate detected a lower percentage of signals and gave many more false alarms, with a greater increase during the session. It would therefore appear

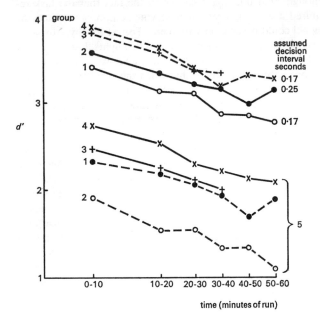

Figure 4 The effect of the assumed decision interval on the levels and slope of d' values. Three different displays were used, with 0, 2 or 12 evenly distributed white marks on the clock face. Values for d' were calculated assuming different lengths of decision interval. Such assumptions varied the level of d' but not the slope (J. F. Mackworth, 1965b)

that this group had a lower sensitivity and a greater decline in sensitivity (d') during the session.

Elliott (1960) pointed out that *auditory* vigilance tasks are more closely 'coupled' than visual ones. By this he meant that with a localized visual display it is not possible for the experimenter to be certain of the nature of the stimulus that reaches the most sensitive area of the retina. Even when eye movement recordings indicate that the subject is looking directly at the signal, the degree of focusing is not known. On the other hand, with an auditory signal fed into the ears by earphones, the nature of the input to the cochlea is much more stable, although there may be changes in the middle ear muscles. This suggestion was examined by Hatfield and Loeb (1968). In order to eliminate the effect of sensory mode, a closely coupled visual task was employed. In this, the subject's eyes were taped shut, and the signal was an increase in intensity of a repetitive light pulse, sufficiently bright to be seen through the closed eyes. In addition, an auditory task and a visual task with open eyes were studied. The event rate was twenty-four per minute, and the signal rate one per minute, with intervals of 10–120 seconds.

There were significant decreases in detections and in false alarms during the session with all conditions. With one signal level, there were significant decreases in d' during the sessions with the closely coupled tasks, both auditory and visual, while the visual task with open eyes showed no significant changes in d' during the session. With three signal levels in one session, there were no significant changes in d' for any of the conditions. There were significant increases in *beta* during the session with each condition. It was found that coupling accounted for a significant part of the variance in seven out of ten possible measures. The authors concluded that the best explanation of the data was in terms of the habituation hypothesis. Irrelevant observing responses in the loosely coupled visual task might inhibit habituation.

Loeb and Binford (1968) examined the effect of various signal to non-signal event ratios in a visual and an auditory task. In contrast to the above results, they found that there was a significant decrement of d' during the sessions with the visual task, but not with the auditory task. There were significant increases in *beta* in the sessions with both modes.

Other tasks showing possible changes in SDT measures

A number of experiments have been reported in which sufficient data have been given to allow the calculations of group values for SDT measures. It has been shown (J. F. Mackworth and Taylor, 1963; J. F. Mackworth, 1964) that values for d' calculated from group data follow much the same course during the session as values calculated for individual subjects. Such group calculations do not, of course, allow determinations of significance levels, unless several groups of subjects have been tested under each condition.

The data shown in Table 1 have been calculated from group data reported by Wilkinson (1964). The signals in an auditory task were shorter tones occurring in a series of regular tones given at a rate of ten per minute. When there were eight signals per hour, detections and false alarms increased during the session. The decrease in d' was from 3·2 at the beginning of the session to 2·3 at the end, while *beta* decreased from 80 to 50, indicating that because there were fewer signals than the subjects were expecting, they adopted a more relaxed criterion. When there were forty-eight signals per hour, there was a fall in false alarms during the session so that *beta* increased from 23 to 111 while d' remained constant at about 2·6. Here there were more signals than the subjects were expecting, and so they adopted a more cautious criterion as time on task proceeded. These changes in false alarms agree with those reported by J. F. Mackworth (1968). The data for d' suggest that even when the event rate is relatively low, there may be changes in d' if the signal rate is sufficiently low. If the signals have an arousing effect, this may counteract the habituation resulting from the repetitive non-signal events, but such an arousal effect of the signals may be insufficient if there are too few signals.

Table 1
The Effect of Knowledge of Results in an Auditory Vigilance Task

Period of Test	8 signals per hr				48 signals per hr											
	No KR				No KR				Part KR				Full KR			
	D	F.A.	d'	beta	D	F.A.	d'	beta	D	F.A.	d'	beta	D	F.A.	d'	beta
1	60	0·17	3·2	80	60	0·6	2·8	23	75	0·5	3·2	22	89	1·7	3·4	4·5
2	30	0·23	2·3	50	51	0·6	2·5	23	75	0·7	3·1	16	89	0·7	3·7	9·6
3	30	0·23	2·3	50	46	0·2	2·8	63	73	0·6	3·1	19	86	0·7	3·5	11·0
4	30	0·23	2·3	50	36	0·1	2·7	111	72	0·7	3·0	17	87	0·9	3·5	8·7

Data taken from Wilkinson (1964)

D = percentage of signals detected.
F.A. = percentage of tones incorrectly given a positive response.
d' = theoretical detectability of signal.
beta = theoretical measure of criterion.

Another experiment which reported false alarm changes during the session as well as detections was one by McGrath (1965). Here both visual and auditory signals were given; the

Table 2
Performance Sharing in an Audio-Visual Task
(Statistics Calculated from McGrath, 1965)

	Single and dual modes combined							
	Visual				Auditory			
Periods	%D	%F.A.	d'	beta	%D	%F.A.	d'	beta
Group I								
Pretest	75	5·0	2·34	3·2	95	2·6	3·89	1·7
Main 1	62	2·6	2·24	6·3	86	1·5	3·25	5·9
2	46	1·6	2·04	9·9	86	0·8	3·49	10·1
3	42	1·6	1·94	9·8	85	0·7	3·49	12·0
Group II								
Pretest	96	0·3	4·50	9·4	67	2·6	2·38	6·0
Main 1	90	0·2	4·16	27·7	48	1·5	2·13	10·5
2	87	0·2	4·00	33·4	43	1·2	2·08	12·6
3	87	0·2	4·00	33·4	46	1·0	2·26	14·9
Means for single mode								
Group I	50	1·8	2·1	9·0	80	0·5	3·42	19·4
Group II	86	0·2	3·96	35·1	48	1·0	2·28	14·9
Means for double mode								
Group I	50	2·3	2·01	7·3	90	1·4	3·48	4·9
Group II	90	0·3	4·03	19·2	45	1·3	2·10	11·7

%D   = percentage of signals detected.

%F.A. = percentage of non-signal events that were given a positive response.

d'   = *the sensitivity of the subject.* The distance between the means of signal and non-signal neural events divided by the standard deviation.

beta = *the criterion of the subject.* The ratio of functions of %D to %F.A.

d' and beta calculated from tables by P. R. Freeman (1964).

repetitive events were tones and lights on for two seconds and off for one second, while the signal was a tone or light of increased intensity. Two levels of signal intensity were used for each mode and combined in such a way that when one mode was easy to detect, the other was difficult. Comparisons were also made with single mode tasks. Table 2 shows the calculations made from the data reported by McGrath. These data combine the single and double presentations except for the whole-session scores. The results show the customary increases in *beta* during the sessions. There was a decrease in *beta* with the dual display as compared with the single display.

Slight decreases in d' appear to have occurred during each session, especially between the pretest and the main run. In the auditory task, there appears to be an increase in d' during the main task. It is interesting to note that while the changes in detections during the sessions were greatest with the more difficult signals, the changes in d' were slightly greater with the easier signals. Changes in *beta* were also greater for the easier signals.

A similar calculation has been carried out by Taylor (1965) on data presented by Wiener *et al.* (1964). Here the events of the task were movements of a voltmeter occurring fifty times a minute. In one condition subjects were asked to add two numbers presented aurally, in addition to the vigilance task. The data showed a marked decrease in d' when the adding task was included, but there were no changes in d' during the sessions. *Beta*, on the other hand, showed its usual increase during all sessions (see Figures 5a, 5b and 5c). Again, the changes in *beta* were greater when the original value was lower, as in the time-sharing task.

Summary and Conclusions

The decrement in detections found during a vigilance task is usually accompanied by a decrease in false alarms, especially in the first session. These changes can be explained on the basis of habituation of the neural and physiological responses to the repetitive events of the task (see p. 16). If the evoked responses to both the signal and non-signal events become reduced, then fewer events of either kind will reach a previously established criterial level. Thus the real criterial level may be unchanged, but detections and false positives will both decrease. In such circumstances there may even be an increase in sensitivity (Weber's law). This increase may, however, be balanced by a decrease in sensitivity due to an increase in the variability of the neural noise (habituation of the arousal responses). In late sessions or in tasks with very rapid or continuous non-signal events this decrease in sensitivity may appear as a decrease in d'.

The apparent change in criterion that is indicated by the decreases in detections and false alarms may also be due to a change in expectancy, especially in the early sessions or following sessions with different signal rates. Such a change in expectancy as to the probability that an event will be a signal can lead directly to a change in criterion, but it can also affect the first level of decision, the decision to make an observation of, or pay attention to, the display (see chapter 4). Thus both expectancy and habituation may alter the observing rate, since habituation of the neural responses to the events may increase the 'cost' or difficulty of paying attention.

3 Division of Attention

The amount of attention paid to a stimulus may vary for two reasons (Hernández-Peón and Sterman, 1966). There is first the dimension of arousal. As a result of increased arousal, either directly produced by the stimulus or for other reasons, the organism may have more attention available to distribute as he chooses (J. F. Mackworth, 1969). The distribution of attention may also vary as the observer, both voluntarily and involuntarily, pays more attention to one or another aspect of the total stimulus input. Such a division of attention is likely to reduce the neural sensitivity of the observer for the unattended stimulus source.

It is important to consider these two dimensions of attention. It has been suggested (Freeman, 1940; Malmo, 1959; Lindsley, 1960) that the relation between the level of arousal and performance is U-shaped. Performance is most efficient at a certain level of drive or arousal, and deteriorates above or below this level. Lindsley points out that the highest level of arousal may be associated with divided attention. The maximum level of performance is associated with the E E G picture of desynchronized random low-amplitude background neural activity. Such a pattern allows maximum discriminability between the stimulus and the neural noise level. With higher levels of arousal, there are increased peripheral physiological changes but no change in neural activity. Therefore, these higher levels may result in interference with the environmental stimuli by the self-generated stimuli. Divided attention may reduce performance at any level of arousal; thus performance may be a resultant of two opposing factors: a direct improvement with decreasing neural noise as a result of higher arousal, and an interference effect due to increasing distraction caused by the physiological manifestations of arousal.

The term distraction is usually employed when the division of attention is involuntary. The effects of noise have been much studied in reference to this concept of distraction. A recent review by Mirabella and Goldstein (1967) concluded that noise might improve or interfere with signal detections, depending on the other factors (see J. F. Mackworth, 1969). Under certain circumstances the interfering effect of noise may become most obvious late in the task, especially in a vigilance task. On the other hand, some authors have found in more active tasks that there may be an initial decrement which later wears off (Harmon, 1933; Hack *et al.*, 1965). Broadbent and Gregory (1965) reported data that suggested that in a vigilance task there were more sure responses at the beginning of the task with noise, but a greater decrement during the session, so that at the end there were fewer unsure positive responses in noise than in quiet. Broadbent (1958) originally suggested that the vigilance decrement was due to an increase in distraction of attention away from the task. The late effect of noise fits in well with this theory. However, he later decided that the vigilance decrement was not due to distraction, as a result of the findings with signal detection measures, and suggested that the effect of noise was to produce a more cautious criterion, the same change produced by time on task in a vigilance experiment (Broadbent and Gregory, 1965).

Division of Attention between Two Relevant Sources

Broadbent (1958) suggested that if a subject is not attending to a stimulus that stimulus is completely rejected and has no effect on him. A. Treisman (1960) suggested, on the other hand, that stimuli that are not attended to are reduced in effective intensity. This is in line with the findings in neuro-physiology that when attention is paid to one set of stimuli the potentials evoked by another set are reduced (see J. F.

Mackworth, 1969; Spong *et al.*, 1965). Broadbent and Gregory (1963a) investigated this question in terms of signal detection theory. Subjects received bursts of noise in one ear, and simultaneously a series of six-item digit sets in the other ear. Half the bursts of noise contained a pure tone. Subjects were asked to indicate on a five-point rating scale at the end of each noise burst their level of certainty as to whether a tone had been present or not. In the condition of divided attention, the subject had to write down the digits before indicating his opinion about the tone.

When the subjects had to divide their attention between the tone and the digits, they reported that they were sure that there was a tone less often than when they listened only for the tone. In addition, they more often reported that there was a tone when there was not, in the condition of divided attention. Thus, there were fewer 'sure' corrects, and more 'sure' false alarms when attention was divided; and d', the measure of discriminability for the tone, was considerably reduced by the requirement to listen to and write down the digits. There was, however, no reliable difference in the criterion, as measured by *beta*. The authors therefore concluded that since these results were so different from those found in vigilance, where the criterion changes and d' often does not, the vigilance decrement cannot be due to diversion of attention from the task (see chapter 4).

Wiener *et al.* (1964) carried out an experiment in which they examined the effect of adding a secondary mental arithmetic task to a vigilance task. The hypothesis was that if the vigilance decrement was a result of decline in arousal, then an extra task should prevent the occurrence of the decrement. They found that the only significant effect was that of time. There was a decline in the percentage of detections of a larger movement of a voltmeter as the session continued. Although there was no significant difference between conditions, least signals were detected in the time-sharing condition (see Figure 5a). Moreover, in this condition there were many more false alarms than in the control conditions.

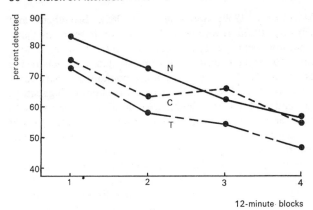

Figure 5a Percentage of signals detected as a function of time in a vigilance task. N=control with auditory numbers, C=control with random noise, T=time sharing task requiring auditory numbers to be added while visual task was performed (Wiener, Poock and Steele, 1964)

Taylor (1965) estimated d' and *beta* from the data reported by Wiener *et al.* and showed that d' was markedly lower in the time-sharing task than with the control conditions (see Figure 5b). This finding agrees with the results reported by Broadbent and Gregory (1963a). While *beta* appeared to increase during the session, the time-sharing group employed a criterion which was considerably less cautious than that employed by the control group (see Figure 5c). Thus, the effect of the time-sharing was the opposite of the effect of time on task. The increase in *beta* during the session was least for the time-sharing group, but maximal for the group who heard the numbers but were not required to do arithmetic. In such a condition, the numbers might have an initial effect in delaying habituation, but since they were irrelevant, the dishabituating effect would soon disappear. This analysis shows that it is important to separate the effects of habituation and division of attention.

Suboski (1966) also found that there was a significant reduction in d' for both visual and auditory detection when these modes were combined. Gould and Schaffer (1967) studied a very complicated multi-channel task and found that with divided attention there was a non-significant decrease in detections and in positive errors. Thus, in terms of *beta* it would appear that the results were the opposite of those reported above when the criterion was more strict with divided attention.

Two Kinds of Signals in the Vigilance Task

A number of workers have examined the effect of presenting signals in two modes, usually auditory and visual. Binford and Loeb (1963) presented the Jump Clock test with ten signals in twenty minutes. Readily detectable auditory signals (half-second increments in a continuous Gaussian noise) were added in numbers ranging from nought to one per minute (eighty in the eighty-minute session). In this experiment with the Clock Test, it was found that false responses to the visual task tended to increase during the session, while detections decreased, even when there were no extra auditory signals.

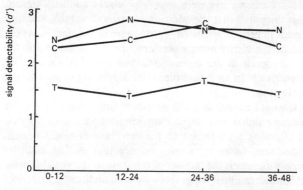

Figure 5b The detectability of the signal during each quarter of the watch for the three groups in Figure 5a (Taylor, 1965)

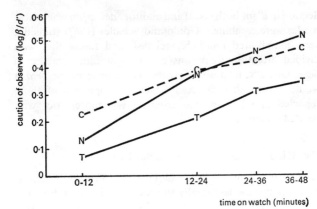

Figure 5c Change over time in the average criterion for the three groups. Criterion plotted as log β/d', time shown on a square root scale (Taylor, 1965)

Thus, the sensitivity of the observer for the double jump must have declined (as measured by d'). Calculating d' values from the data reported, d' for the visual signals in the initial twenty minutes was 4·1 when there were no auditory signals, and 4·5 and 4·4 when there were twenty or eighty auditory signals. This suggested that the addition of easily detectable auditory signals improved sensitivity for the rare visual signals. At the end of the eighty-minute sessions, the values for d' for the visual signals in the three conditions were 3·6, 3·6 and 3·7 respectively. In each case there was a decrease in *beta* during the session.

It would appear that the dishabituating effect of the extra auditory signals outweighed any interference due to division of attention with regard to the detection of visual signals. There was, however, some evidence that adding auditory signals increased the latency of response to the visual signals, which was minimal when there were no auditory signals. But when there were auditory signals, the latency of the visual signals decreased as the number of auditory signals increased. Maximal visual latency, especially towards the end of the session, was found with the twenty auditory signals. These results suggest that the dishabituating effect of auditory signals increased as the number of signals increased, though there was an interference due to having to pay attention to the auditory mode. It was also found that false visual responses occurred most often with the greater numbers of auditory signals, though false responses in general were very few.

Buckner and McGrath (1963a) also reported an experiment in which signals were presented on both auditory and visual channels. When the signals were presented on both modes simultaneously, being regarded as one signal, there was a considerable improvement in detection in this redundant condition. When the signal appeared independently on the two channels, there was a slight improvement in detection of the easy auditory signals, and a decrease in detection of the difficult visual signals. McGrath (1965) expanded this experiment, combining difficult and easy signals in either mode, and comparing the results with single channel tasks. The data have been presented in Table 2 to which have been added calculations of the statistics d' and $beta$. The effects of adding an extra channel requiring simultaneous attention appear to have been as follows:

1. With the dual mode, detections tended to increase for the easy signals and decrease slightly for the difficult ones. Very small changes in d' in the same direction may also be seen in Table 2.

2. There was an increase in false alarms for both levels of difficulty in each mode, when the modes were combined. Subjects apparently maintained detection performance at the expense of more positive errors.

The increase in false alarms as a result of divided attention appears to be a fairly consistent finding. This is in contrast to the usual finding of a decrease in false alarms occuring during a vigilance task.

J. F. Mackworth (1963a) examined the effect of presenting two kinds of signals on the Continuous Clock. The Clock face was divided into alternating black and white segments. When signals were expected only on the black segments, performance was better than when signals were expected on both kinds of segment, even though the total number of signals was increased. When the number of white signals was increased (J. F. Mackworth and Taylor, 1963) there was a further decrease in detection of the black signals, and also a decrease in false alarms. There appeared to be some reduction in sensitivity (d') for the black signals as a result of increasing the white signals, but sensitivity for the white signals was increased by increasing their number, suggesting that more attention was being paid to the white signals and less to the black signals.

In each case (Broadbent and Gregory, 1963a; Wiener *et al.*, 1964; McGrath, 1965; J. F. Mackworth and Taylor, 1963) it was the more difficult or less probable signal that showed the decrease in detectability. C. H. Baker and Harabedian (1962) combined an auditory vigilance task of two levels of difficulty with a visual tracking task. Addition of the tracking task reduced detections in the auditory task. This effect was most powerful in the alerted pretest, and when the main watches were analysed alone, the effect of the tracking task was not significant. In the pretest the effect of the tracking task was greatest with the difficult auditory signal, though this was not true for the main watch. With the easy auditory task alone, detections actually improved during the session. Again, the data suggest that division of attention is most harmful when the subject is fully alert. At a lower level of alertness, the extra task may help to maintain alertness.

Bergum and Lehr (1963c) reported an experiment in which the subjects were required to respond to readily discriminable secondary visual or auditory signals. No significant differences were found between conditions, but performance on the main task was poorer when the extra task was present, especially at the beginning of the session.

C. H. Baker (1961) reported an experiment in which division of attention had no harmful effect. In this experiment, it was emphasized to the subjects that the vigilance task was the primary task, and that if signals occurred on the secondary task, they would be less frequent than signals on the main task. They were also told that feedback on their performance on the secondary task would indicate to them how well they were performing the main task. There was a marked improvement in performance on the main task when the secondary signals were expected, even before any such signal had been presented. It therefore appeared that the motivating or arousing effect of expecting to receive information on their performance was more powerful than any interference due to division of attention.

Glucksberg (1963) also investigated the effect of adding a tracking task to a detection task, but in this case, the tracking task was the main one. The signals on the detection task were well above threshold. Visual signals interfered with the visual tracking task, while auditory and cutaneous signals did not. The latency of response to all signal modes was increased, when the tracking task was added. When, however, the detection task required a more difficult discrimination, there was a much smaller change in latency due to tracking. This finding is contrary to those reported above.

Poulton (1966) has discussed work relating to division of attention. He pointed out that the addition of an extra task may reveal differences between tasks which are both too easy to show differences when tested alone. It is necessary to saturate the capacity of the subject in order to reveal a deterioration due to added load.

Antrobus and Singer (1964) examined detection of brightness changes in a two-hour session, during which the subject was required either to talk with the experimenter or to count aloud. In a further test eight three-minute trials were given under each condition with band music between the trials. Detections were significantly fewer with talking. The authors argued that with high arousal, subject-generated cognitive stimuli interfered with signal detection, but with low arousal, interference and arousal counteracted each other. This suggestion agrees with much of the data presented above.

Bakan and Manley (1963) reported an experiment that would appear to be related to division of attention. They compared the detection of auditory signals by subjects who were blindfolded with detection by normal subjects. They found that the sighted males detected significantly fewer signals than the blindfolded males, who detected about the same number of signals as did females, whether sighted or blindfolded.

Kerstin and Eysenck (1965) and Eysenck and Thompson (1966) examined the effect of adding a secondary discrimination task to the pursuit rotor task, and found that even when the signals on the secondary task were rare, performance on the rotor was lowered. There was a linear relation between performance decrement and signal rate. While the group with no distraction showed a decrement during the session, the subjects with the extra task showed an improvement. After a ten-minute rest, all groups were the same; thus, it would appear that distraction did not interfere with learning the task, but only with immediate performance.

R. L. Smith *et al.* (1966) examined the effect of adding a compatible secondary task to a vigilance task. The vigilance task consisted of a paper tape that showed 900 'noise' squares per hour. The signal was a square with an arm in the centre of one side. The secondary task required the solving of anagrams. The addition of this secondary task greatly increased the number of signals that were detected. In fact, the performance with the secondary task was as good as performance in a condition in which a buzzer was sounded one second before a signal appeared. Here the alerting or dishabituating effect of solving anagrams appeared to have been considerable. All conditions tended to show an improvement during the session, indicating that the subjects were learning to discriminate the signal from the 'noise'.

Capacity

Attention may be divided, not merely between two different sources of stimuli, but also between the different aspects of a particular task. J. F. Mackworth (1963c, 1964, 1966) found that there was a direct relationship between the rate at which items of different kinds or material could be named and the number of such items that could be recalled from short-term memory. Thus, digits were read most rapidly and most digits were recalled, while shapes were named slowly and received the poorest recall. It was proposed that attention had to be divided between the coding or naming of the material and maintaining it in memory. It was found, in accordance with this hypothesis, that the amount of material lost from memory as a result of reading other material was proportional to the difficulty of naming the interfering material. The effect of coding difficulty was a constant, and not dependent on the number of items.

A number of papers in the Symposium on Attention and Performance at Soesterberg in 1966 (Sanders, 1967) dealt with the concept that the observer has a limited capacity which has to be shared among the various operations that he is attempting to carry out simultaneously. Moray (1967) suggested that the capacity of the brain could be divided among the incoming information from various sources, the transforms performed on this material, and the output operations. When subjects were highly practised, less capacity was necessary for the two latter functions so that there was an apparent expansion of capacity for the intake of information. To this formulation should be added the process of retaining the material in storage until required; that is, short term memory. Attention and capacity are similar concepts. When a stimulus of completely known parameters is received, it is quickly dealt with by the already established programme or model, and excites only the small local area of the brain that is necessary for putting this programme into action. But when a stimulus of unknown parameters is received, it excites a much larger area of the brain, producing tonic arousal, or widespread evoked potentials, while a model or programme is constructed. This process interferes with storage, and delays the response.

Taylor *et al.* (1967) suggested that the capacity could be

measured by determining the detectability, d'_s, of a signal when presented alone, and its detectability, d'_m, when another task is being performed at the same time. 'The processor capacity devoted to the task in the shared environment is d'^2_m/d'^2_s, times the capacity used for the single task alone.' Taylor *et al.* quoted experiments in which a dot and a tone burst were presented simultaneously. The subjects were required to detect two aspects of each stimulus. It was found that the sharing index, the sum of the sharing ratios d'^2_m/d'^2_s, was 0·85 in all cases. Division of attention between two aspects of one modality produced the same difficulty as dividing attention between two modalities. It was suggested that the remaining 15 per cent of the capacity was employed in the programming required to monitor the sharing procedure.

Tulving and Lindsay (1967) described similar experiments. They presented simultaneous circles and tones. Information transmission was increased with duration of the stimulus, decreased with simultaneous presentation as compared with single presentation, and less in the secondary modality than in the primary. It was found that even when the visual stimuli were exposed for two seconds there was still a considerable impairment in performance with simultaneous auditory presentation. Since stimulus intensity had no effect on visual identification, it would seem that if there was 'attenuation' of information, it was not a simple reduction in intensity. Nor did the data support the sequential processing of information.

Summary and Conclusions

There is considerable evidence that the alerted brain has a limited capacity for dealing with incoming stimuli. This capacity must be divided between the various stimuli of importance, the coding and memorizing of the data, and the output. Attention can be voluntarily turned from one to another aspect of the stimulus situation, and within this alteration of attention goes an alteration in the size of the neural potential evoked by the stimulus to which attention is being paid. The ability to 'tune-out' an unwanted stimulus is of considerable importance to the organism, as it results in freeing the decision-making capacity for vital decisions. Once programmes have been completely established for dealing with a particular stimulus with a particular response, or, in other words, once an activity is fully learned, it no longer requires so much attention. Once we have learned to walk, some lower part of the brain takes care of all the myriad adjustments to the terrain, and even takes us on our accustomed route with no awareness of how we manage to reach our destination, while considering an important problem.

While both the vigilance decrement and time-sharing result in reduced detections, and also in reduced amplitude of evoked potentials, there appear to be differences in the false alarms. These tend to decrease in a vigilance task and to increase in a time-sharing task. It is possible that at least some of the changes in false alarms are related to changes in expectancy. In vigilance tasks, subjects may find that there are fewer signals than they were expecting, and therefore become more cautious, while in the time-shared task, they may realize that they are missing signals as a result of paying attention to the other task, and therefore adopt a more relaxed criterion. Divided attention produces a marked decrease in sensitivity (d'), in contrast to most vigilance tasks.

4 Observing Responses and the Event Rate

One of the most important findings in vigilance research has been the discovery that the probability that a signal will be detected is considerably reduced when the background event rate is increased. N. H. Mackworth (1957) suggested that the event rate, the rate of *unwanted* signals, might be an important aspect of the vigilance decrement. 'A regular repetition of unwanted signals that the man is trying to neglect is just as harmful for alertness as is the irregularity in time for the wanted signals' (1957, p. 391). He pointed out that, 'Research is needed on these three aspects of the unwanted signal – regularity, frequency and similarity.' Very little work has as yet been carried out on regularity and similarity of the unwanted and wanted signals, but the effect of the *frequency of the unwanted signals* has received increasing attention.

For good performance, a subject has to make a decision about each event in a vigilance task. In order to do this, he has to pay attention to each event. The main hypothesis of this book is that the decrement in detections or speed of response in a vigilance task is related to habituation of the neural responses to these events, in addition to the reduction of the level of arousal due to the monotony of the environment. The expectancy that an event will be a signal will also be affected by the ratio of unwanted to wanted signals. It has been found, however, that the event rate may affect performance independently of the signal to non-signal event ratio.

Holland (1957) suggested that the techniques employed in operant conditioning of animals could be useful in analysing the 'observing responses' of humans in a vigilance task (see Skinner, 1938). He defined these observing responses as 'looking at' or 'orienting to' the display. In so far as the observing response is an overt movement, the concept would seem to be limited to visual displays, and even there little evidence has been produced to support the suggestion. Considered as an orienting response, however, which may perhaps be redefined as 'paying attention' to the display, the suggestion has had valuable results. For it is clear that for good performance each event in the task must receive attention, and therefore the required rate of 'observing responses' is the same as the event rate. The concept of 'attention' remains as inaccessible as ever, though its concomitants can be measured as neural or other physiological changes. Perhaps the most valuable idea to come of this suggestion is that vigilance tasks involve *two* stages of decision, the first stage being the decision whether or not to 'observe' the display, and the second the decision whether or not to make a positive response to the observed event. It is clear that the 'observing response' has much in common with the orienting response discussed by Sokolov (1963); see also J. F. Mackworth (1969).

Holland (1957) examined a situation in which the subjects were required to press a key in order to illuminate the display for 0·07 seconds. The signal was a deflection of a dial pointer, which remained deflected until the subject reset it. Subjects began to press the key about a minute before they expected the signal to occur, and they continued pressing it at a high rate until the signal occurred. After the signal there was a pause, the length of which was determined by the expected interval. Signals were presented at regular intervals.

In a later experiment, Holland (1963) studied observing behaviour with a variable interval, ranging from five seconds to six minutes. All four human subjects showed periods of lower observing rates in the later parts of the session. Reinforcement by signal detection was insufficient to maintain the high initial rate which resulted from the subject's past experience. In a final experiment, Holland presented transient signals with the intervals used by N. H. Mackworth (1950), ranging from thirty seconds to ten minutes. Holland found that nearly half the subjects detected all but one of the signals. The observing rate displayed by these subjects actually increased during the session. The rest of the subjects showed a reduction in the observing rate and in detections later in the session. Holland suggested that the missing of signals led to a lowering of the apparent signal rate, with a consequent lowering of the observing response rate. Since the transient nature of the signals gave a differential reinforcement to high observing rates, the active subjects became more active and the inactive ones less active. (See also Laties and Weiss, 1960.)

Blair (1958) modified this experiment by attaching the light that illuminated the display to the head of the observer. Thus the display was only lit when the observer was facing it. He found that while some subjects displayed the scallop-shaped curve that Holland had found, others observed the display continuously. Since there was little or no difficulty involved in sitting facing a display, there was no particular reason why the subjects should not have made this continuous observing response. C. H. Baker (1960a) photographed his subjects while they were monitoring the Jump Clock, and found that in only one case was a subject not observing the display when a signal occurred. There was no correlation between the number of times that a subject was observing the display and the general activity of the subject, and her detection performance. This made it clear that the gross observing response of looking towards the display was not related to detection performance.

J. F. Mackworth and N. H. Mackworth (1958a) reported that a study of eye-fixations showed that subjects could be looking directly at a required target and not notice it. N. H. Mackworth et al. (1964) showed that in a vigilance situation every missed signal was fixated, when only one dial was used. It can be concluded that the vigilance decrement is probably not related to an overt observing response. When two dials were used, most of the unreported signals were not fixated. Those who shifted their gaze most often between the dials detected most signals. Moreover similar decrements have been found in auditory tasks, which in humans are more closely coupled, in the sense that there is seldom an overt change aimed at the source of signals.

Jerison and Wing (1961) reported a study of observing responses in the Jump Clock Test. In one session, subjects had to press a key to light the display, while in the other there was normal illumination. Introducing the illumination response reduced the absolute number of detections but left the shape of the decrement curve unchanged. Although there was a significant correlation between illumination responses and detections in the same session, the correlation between illumination responses and detections in the other, normally-lit session, was not significant. They therefore concluded that the illumination response rate was not related to the vigilance factor.

Broadbent (1963a) also studied instrumental observing responses. Each time that the observer pressed a switch, three lights flashed. The signal was a failure of one light to flash. The rate of observing responses increased during the session, as Holland had found with his good subjects. There was, however, an increase in the latency of detection concomitant with the increasing rate of observing responses.

Jerison and Pickett (1963) mentioned that Holland's results could only be obtained when the illumination switch was hard to operate. Dardano (1965) made a study of observing behaviour in relation to conditioning techniques. The subject had to press a switch loaded with 100 gms in order to illuminate the display for 0·1 second. The signal was a deflection of the needle of a voltmeter, which either remained until response was made, or else disappeared after about 1.2 seconds, at which point either a bell rang or a shock was delivered to the subject. These latter conditions were known as limited hold. Each group received alternating periods of limited hold and the other condition. The observing response rate was increased by both kinds of limited hold, the shock having the bigger effect. There was however no carry-over from the shock periods to the intervening periods without limited hold.

Thus, the observing response rate could not be permanently affected by the experimental variables. The most obvious component of the human orienting response is the line of sight. Although failure to detect a signal may occur even when the subject is looking directly at it, failure is even more probable if he is not looking at the exact spot where the signal occurs. The evoked response to a stimulus is considerably affected by the area of the retina on which the stimulus falls (Eason *et al.*, 1967, J. F. Mackworth, 1969). *Measurements of the line of sight, the neural responses and performance must all be made simultaneously before any adequate hypothesis of the causes of the decrement can be achieved.* A useful approach to this problem is found in some studies in progress on the initial orienting and habituation of eye fixations on a novel and unique element in a display (N. H. Mackworth and Otto, in press).

Twenty children (two to five years old) were asked to look at a series of displays, presenting a 4×4 matrix of simple geometric symbols (circles, squares, etc.). They were left free to study these displays in any way they wished. Each display was presented ten times in a series of three-second trials, separated by five-second pauses. A new wide-angle reflection eye-camera was used to record the visual choices, as indicated by the position of the gaze on the display. This eye-camera takes a direct close-up of the right eye, with the display reflected in the pupil (N. H. Mackworth, 1968). The centre of the pupil marks the location of the gaze on the display. No bite bar is required with this equipment, only a headrest.

The first display presented sixteen white symbols on a black background. Immediately after the ten trials with this display, the presentation was replaced by one in which one of the two circles was coloured red, and all the other symbols were unchanged. After twenty trials with this red circle, it returned to white for the final ten trials.

An analysis was made of the percentage of movie frames in which the gaze rested on the test circle. When the circle changed to red 65 per cent of all observing responses were

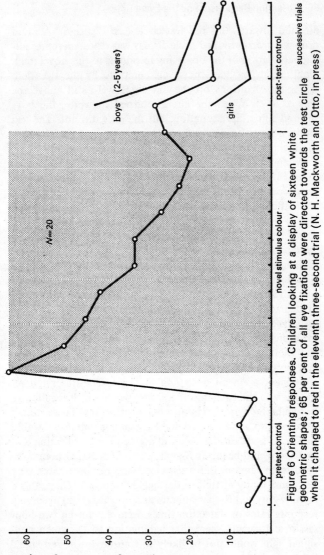

Figure 6 Orienting responses. Children looking at a display of sixteen white geometric shapes; 65 per cent of all eye fixations were directed towards the test circle when it changed to red in the eleventh three-second trial (N. H. Mackworth and Otto, in press)

directed towards this red test circle (see Figure 6). A rapid drop was seen as the red circle display was repeated, representing habituation of the observing responses to this novel item. Habituation was not, however, complete by the twentieth trial, since fixations on the red circle were still above the chance level. When the circle returned to white, the boys showed some dishabituation, but the girls did not. The test circle, now white, was still attracting more than its fair share of the children's attention by the end of the experiment.

When the red circle first appeared, the children were able to locate it by peripheral vision, since the second fixation usually rested on this novel item. The children considered the red circle thoughtfully in relatively long stares; the gaze lingered on the circle for periods of one to two seconds. In the initial control display, the average fixation lasted for only about one-third of a second.

Mention should be made here of animal studies designed to simulate the vigilance situation (see J. F. Mackworth, 1969). In such studies the detection response is usually reinforced immediately by food. These experiments would therefore come into the category of knowledge of results and reward, so that the decrement found in human experiments is unlikely to occur. De Lorge *et al.* (1967) examined the behaviour of squirrel monkeys in a task in which the presentation of stimuli was contingent upon an observing response. The observing response was the pressing of a lever switch which resulted in a stimulus light appearing on a push-button key. These stimuli were of two kinds, a red light signalling that food would follow pressure on the key, and a green light, indicating that no food would be given. Signal rates of 7·5–60 per hour were used, with random intervals. Observing response rates were not consistently related to the signal frequency. They ranged from twenty to fifty per minute, and no changes in observing response rates or detection times occurred during two-hour sessions. It would seem that habituation to the green non-signal light would not be likely to transfer to the red signal light.

Event Rate

Colquhoun (1961) followed up the suggestion by N. H. Mackworth (1957) that the nature and frequency of the 'unwanted' signals might be important in a vigilance task. J. F. Mackworth and N. H. Mackworth (1958b) had found that performance in a search task was considerably affected by the amount of 'unwanted' material present in the display. Colquhoun suggested that the probability of detection of a signal might be dependent on the probability that an event was a signal. He used a task in which the event was a strip displaying six green discs. The 'wanted' signal was a paler disc. Two event rates were studied, 144 and twenty-four strips in the forty minutes of the task. These event rates represent rates of 3·6 or 0·6 strips per minute, rates that are unusually slow for vigilance tasks. Each strip of discs was visible for two seconds. The numbers of events (strips) presenting a signal were twelve or seventy-two in forty minutes, representing signal rates of 1·8 or 0·3 per minute. Thus, the probability that there would be a signal on a strip was either 0·5 (12/24 or 72/144) or 0·08 (12/144). The variability of the signal interval was kept low.

The results showed that detection efficiency was related only to the probability that there would be a signal on a strip. Subjects detected a smaller percentage of signals from the condition with twelve signals and 144 events than from the other two conditions, which were not significantly different from each other. Significant decrements, however, occurred only with the high signal probability of 0·5 (see Figure 7).

Colquhoun found that the difference between the conditions was mainly due to a failure to detect the signals when they occurred in the peripheral position on the strip. Jerison (1966) suggested that the reduction in signal probability might produce a change in visual search patterns rather than an alteration in detection ability. Colquhoun (1966b) repeated the experiment with two discs per strip as well as six discs. He found that the low (0·08) signal probability reduced detection with both numbers of discs, but that there was now no interaction between locations and the effect of the signal probability. Detection was substantially higher with the two-disc strips than with the six-disc strips. Thus, detection of signals from the two-disc strips was higher with the 0·08 signal probability than detection of signals from the six-disc strips with the

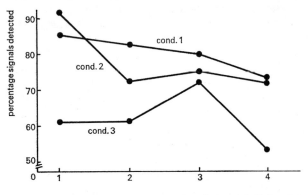

Figure 7 Average detection efficiency over all signal positions in successive ten-minute periods of a visual vigilance task. Condition 1 : 72 signal strips and 72 non-signal strips in 40 minutes ; Condition 2 : 12 of each kind ; Condition 3 : 12 signal strips and 132 non-signal strips (Colquhoun, 1961)

0·5 signal probability. In the first case the total number of discs was 288, while in the second case there were 864 discs, and the ratios of signal to non-signal *discs* were 0·04 and 0·08 respectively. It is clear that in these experiments the probability that an event (a disc) would be a signal determined the overall probability of detection.

Weiner and Ross (1962) studied the effect of 'unwanted' signals upon observing responses. When the subjects pressed a lever, a light might appear. The signal was a red light, while the 'unwanted' signal (or non-signal event) was a different coloured light. Each event, either signal or 'unwanted' signal, remained available until an observing response was made. The signal rate (24 per hour) and the intersignal interval were those employed by N. H. Mackworth (1950). The 'unwanted' signals appeared at rates of 0·5, 1 or 4 per minute, with either regular or irregular intervals. There was also a condition where an unwanted signal appeared at every lever press, unless a signal was scheduled.

The dependent variable was the rate of observing responses (OR). There was a considerable increase in OR as the rate of 'unwanted' signals increased, and also when the interval between unwanted signals was variable. Amphetamine produced an increase in the rate of OR.

Changes during the session were complex. There was a decrease in OR with no unwanted signals and with regular unwanted signals at 0·5 per minute, while there was an increase during the sessions with the higher unwanted signal rates. The rate of OR was extremely high, varying from one OR in 1·5 seconds, found at the end of the sessions with the lowest unwanted signal rate, to seven OR per second, found towards the end of sessions with other conditions. The authors pointed out that the unwanted signals were clearly acting as a reinforcement. The results are similar to what might be expected if the 'unwanted' signals had been wanted.

McGrath (1963a) described a task in which the event rate was varied. With the fast rate, a light came on for one-third of a second and was off for two-thirds. In the slow rate, the light was on for one second, and off for two seconds. The signal was an increment in the brightness of the light. Thus, the duration of the signal was changed with the event rate. Performance was considerably better with the slow event rate, even in the alerted pre- and post-tests. The two rates were tested under two conditions of ambient audio stimulation (see J. F. Mackworth, 1969). There was no significant difference in the overall decrement between the two event rates, but there was a marked interaction between the event rates and the ambient conditions.

Jerison and Pickett (1963) enlarged the concept of the observing response in relation to the vigilance task. They suggested that there are *two kinds of observing responses*, the first being the orientation of the observer towards the display, and the second being the selection of messages by physiological changes in the central nervous system. While the first kind of observing is mainly limited to a visual display, the second kind is related to all modes of vigilance tasks. When attention is paid to a stimulus, the neural response to that stimulus, the evoked potential, is enhanced (Spong *et al.*, 1965; J. F. Mackworth, 1969). At the same time, the background neural 'noise' is inhibited, so that the sensitivity for the stimulus is increased. Other physiological changes, such as pupil enlargement, or tightening of the muscles of the ear, may also increase sensitivity. As yet, however, very little is known about the very important process of attention.

Jerison and Pickett assumed that in a vigilance detection task, if the observer is not paying attention to the display at the time when a signal appears, he will not report the signal. This may be extended to latency tasks, where the signal is easy to detect. If the observer is not paying attention to the display, either visual or auditory, when the signal is presented, the latency of the response will be increased. They suggested that the decision of the observer to make an observation of the display would depend upon the relative costs and rewards of making an observation. The analysis depended on the assumption that the effort of making an observation has a definite cost. The second assumption was that this cost of an observation would increase as the task proceeded. It can be seen that the discussion was independent of any theories as to why the cost would increase. The authors suggested that the cost might be due to two factors. Firstly, there would be a build-up of inhibition resulting from paying attention to the repetitive series of events, so few of which were signals, and secondly, there might be a positive reward associated with paying attention to matters other than the task. This might involve looking at or listening to events unrelated to the task, or else paying attention mainly to inner thoughts. The concept of inhibition has been discussed by J. F. Mackworth (1969). If inhibition of the neural response to the repetitive events of the display has arisen, then paying attention to something other than these events may dissipate this inhibition. A third possibility is that moments of drowsiness may also dissipate inhibition, providing an effective rest pause even though the eyes are apparently resting on the display.

The relative costs or utility values of the various outcomes of the decision whether or not to observe can be altered in two main ways. The first way involves the neural changes already discussed. It is probable that a certain level of arousal is actively sought by most higher organisms, though this level may vary considerably at different times of day. There are areas of the brain which have been demonstrated to be actively rewarding. When electrodes are implanted in these areas, the subject will stimulate itself continuously (Olds and Milner, 1954). Though these areas are not identical with the areas particularly associated with arousal, it is reasonable to imagine that they may also be stimulated by the generalized effects of arousal. It has been demonstrated that rats will inject themselves with a regular dose of amphetamine, varying their injection rate with the dose level, so that the amount of the drug which they self-administer is kept constant (Pickens *et al.*, 1967; J. F. Mackworth, 1969). This strongly suggests that a certain level of stimulus arousal is highly rewarding. The great part played in human history by the various drugs that stimulate or depress emphasizes the importance of this factor of arousal.

The second way in which the utilities of the outcomes of the decision to observe can be altered is by changes in the outlook of the subject. His estimates of the probability of the signal, his attitude to the importance of not missing a signal or to the importance of not making a false positive error, immediate reward and punishment in the form of knowledge of results, all can affect his estimates of the values and costs of both levels of decision, the observing response and the decision whether or not to make an overt response. The attitude of the subject may range all the way from 'couldn't care less', which may express itself in overt sleep, to a feverish anxiety to do well. Since in a vigilance task the ratio of signal to non-signal events may be around 1–120 or less, a very low cost of an observation of a non-signal event may easily outweigh a reward a hundred times greater than is attached to the observation and detection of a signal. The ability of the subject to predict when there will be a signal, or at least when there is very unlikely to be a signal, will have a considerable effect on his decision whether or not to observe. When he knows that there is not likely to be a signal within twenty or thirty seconds of the last one, he can take an effective rest, and return his attention to the display.

Thus, changes in the observing rate during the session may be due to changes in the expectancy of the subject or to changes in the cost of observing. The second decision process concerns whether or not to make a positive response to an observation. This is the decision process which has been investigated in detail in signal detection experiments. Given a particular sensory event, the decision of the observer to give a positive response rests upon many of the factors mentioned above, such as his estimates of the probability of the signal, the relative importance of hits and false alarms and so on. The adoption of a very strict criterion by the observer may give the same result as the absence of an observation, due to the fact that the observer was not paying attention to the display. The difference between these two states is, however, of considerable interest to the theoretical scientist.

Jerison *et al.* (1965) discussed the two stages of decision in a vigilance task in greater detail (see Figures 8a, b and c). They reported that when the event rate was increased from five to thirty events per minute, with fifteen signals per hour, the initial probability of detection of the signals was decreased from 0·9 to 0·6. The decrement in detection during the session was also greater with the higher event rate, so that the final probability of detection was 0·8 with the low event rate and 0·3 with the high event rate. There was, however, no significant difference in the detectability of the signal, as measured by d', between the two conditions, nor within a session. This was because the probability of a false alarm decreased concomitantly with the detection probability. It must be emphasized that even if there were no differences in the number of false alarms in the two conditions, there would be a

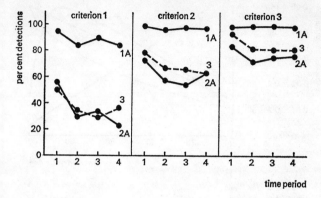

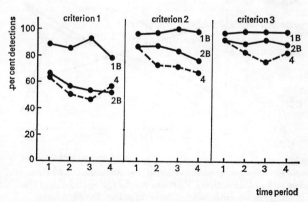

Figure 8a Mean percentage of detected signals in a visual vigilance task. Condition 1 : 20 signals in 400 events. Condition 2 : 20 signals in 2400 events. Condition 3 : 40 signals. Condition 4 : 20 signals in 4800 events. Criterion 1, 2, 3 refer to experimenter's criterion of a detection

considerable reduction in the probability that a non-signal event would receive a positive response with the faster event rate. (It was found by J. F. Mackworth, 1968a, that in two tasks

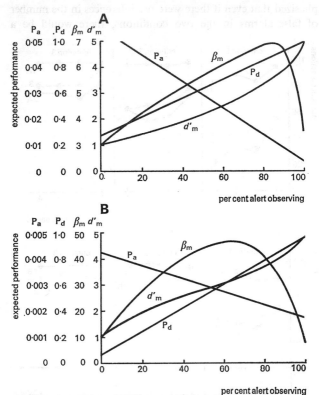

Figure 8b A heuristic model relating measured values of P_d (probability of detection), P_a (false alarms), d'_m and β_m to the percentage of time that 'alert' observing occurs during a vigil. A. Mixture of 'alert' ($d' = 5 \cdot 0$, $\beta = 3 \cdot 0$) with 'blurred' ($d' = 1 \cdot 0$, $\beta = 3 \cdot 0$) observing appropriate for Condition 1. B. Mixture of 'alert' ($d' = 5 \cdot 0$, $\beta = 8 \cdot 5$) and 'blurred' ($d' = 1 \cdot 0$, $\beta = 8 \cdot 5$) observing appropriate to Conditions 3 and 4

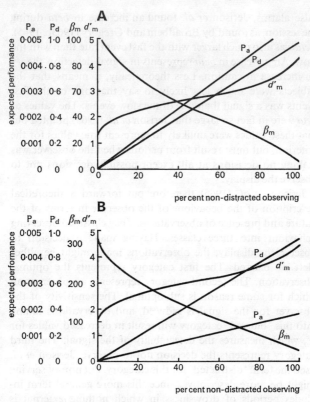

Figure 8c A heuristic model relating measured values of P_d, P_a, d'_m and β_m to the percentage of the time that non-distracted observing (95 per cent 'alert' observing) occurs. Distraction is defined as the time during which no information is taken from the display and no responses (detections or false alarms) are emitted. A. Model appropriate for Condition 1. B. Model appropriate for Conditions 3 and 4 (Jerison, Pickett and Stenson, 1965)

with quite different event rates, the actual number of false alarms was dependent only on the signal rate.)

As a consequence of the reduction in detections and in

false alarms, Jerison *et al.* found an increase in *beta* during the session, as found by Broadbent and Gregory (1963b, 1965). *Beta* was also much larger with the fast event rate than with the slow. An increase in *beta* represents in signal detection theory an increase in caution. Less theoretically, it means that the subjects were much less likely to say that one of the fast events was a signal than one of the slow events. The values of *beta* were in fact so large that Jerison *et al.* (1965) pointed out that these values were unlikely to represent true values for the criterion, but must result from periods when the observer was making no decisions at all, except possibly decisions not to observe the display.

Jerison *et al.* (1965) therefore put forward a theoretical description of the behaviour of the observer in terms of the nature and presence of observations. They classified observing behaviour into three classes. Having made a decision to observe the display, the observations made might be either alert or blurred. The first category represents the optimal observation. The second category represents an observation which for some reason is sub-optimal. The sensitivity of the observer for the signal is reduced, and observations falling into this 'blurred' category will result in decreased values for d', which measures the detectability of the signal. The third category represents the decision not to observe. Jerison *et al.* used the term 'distracted' for this category, but non-observing might be more descriptive, since this more general term includes periods of drowsiness in which nothing external is being observed. These three categories lead to a three-dimensional model of vigilance (see Figures 8b and 8c).

The authors illustrated the complicated relationships that might arise with different proportions of the various kinds of observing behaviour. They pointed out, however, that the probability of detection should show a linear relation with the proportion of alert observing, and therefore concluded that the alteration of the percentage of detections during a vigilance session is due to changes in observing behaviour. If observing behaviour is considered to include the physiological and neural changes already considered, then this conclusion is in agreement with the main hypothesis of this book, though the vigilance decision not to 'observe', which may be the decision to inhibit the physiological response to the stimulus, cannot be regarded as exactly voluntary.

Jerison *et al.* (1965) did not find a reliable decrement in d' during the session, although there was a reliable increase in *beta*. In this finding they agreed with other authors. J. F. Mackworth and Taylor (1963) did find a reliable decrement in d' with the Continuous Clock, and J. F. Mackworth (1965c) found a decrement in sensitivity when the background events were flashes of light at 200 per minute, but not when the flash rate was forty per minute. It was concluded that continuous or very fast visual changes could lead to blurred observing. A similar situation might have been present in the experiment by Stern (1966) where the signal was a small movement of a steady light. He suggested that the very high false alarm rate might have been due to autokinetic movements.

J. F. Mackworth (unpublished) tested two event rates with the Jump Clock. The small decrements in d' were not significant, but there was a significantly smaller number of signals detected with the faster event rate. There was also a greater decrease in false alarms during the session with this fast event rate, so that there was a considerably greater change in *beta* than with the slow event rate. It has been suggested that this might be due to the decreased neural response to the events, both signal and non-signal. In such a case, if the criterion remained at the same level of neural event as before, then both kinds of events would receive fewer positive responses (see Table 3).

Jerison (1967a, b, c) has described further experiments investigating the effect of the event rate on detection. He found that it was not only a question of signal probability, because relatively low probability signals (0·01) were detected as rarely as 30 per cent of the time or as often as 80 per cent depending on the non-signal stimulus frequency (see Figure 9).

In the first case, the event rate was 1800 per hour, while in the second case, the event rate was at or below 600 events per hour. With the low event rate, essentially the whole vigilance effect disappeared. There was no decrement and no effect of signal frequency, while with the high stimulus rate, both the decrement and an effect of signal frequency were found. This is the result that would be expected if the decrement is due to

Table 3

The Effect of Jump Rate on Percentage of Signals Detected, False Alarms and SDT Measures (30 Signals Per Hour)

Period (mins)	120 jumps per minute				30 jumps per minute			
	% Detected	% F.A.	d'	Beta	% Detected	% F.A.	d'	Beta
0–20	69	0·55	3·07	22	72	1·6	2·74	8·5
20–40	56	0·32	2·87	41	71	1·4	2·76	10·0
40–60	54	0·22	2·92	57	64	1·4	2·56	10·0

habituation, since the rate of habituation is closely dependent on the event rate (see Figure 9).

Loeb and Binford (1968) also varied the signal rate and the event rate independently, in a visual and an auditory task. Signal rates were one-half, one, or two per minute, and event rates were six, twelve and twenty-four pulses per minute. It was found that there were significant differences in detections between event rates and over time. The signal rate did not have a significant effect on visual detections but did affect auditory detections. False alarms showed a decrease during only one of the visual sessions, that with the lowest signal and carrier rates, but with the auditory task there were more false alarms, and a more consistent decrease during the session. For a constant *signal to non-signal ratio*, auditory detections were higher at the lower event rates, though visual detections were not significantly different within each ratio. Percentage detections were lower with lower ratios for each mode.

The detectability of the signal, as measured by d', decreased as the event rate increased from twelve to twenty-four per minute. *Beta*, the measure of the strictness of the criterion, increased with an increase in the event rate. There were significant differences between signal to non-signal ratios for

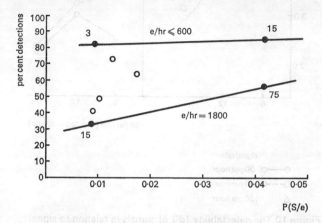

Figure 9 Detection performance during the final hour of an 80-minute vigil as a function of probability of signal given stimulus event, P(S/e). Lines connect groups that are the same with respect to stimulus events per hour (e/hr). Numbers indicate signals per hour (Jerison, 1967)

both measures, and also some variation within ratios, especially for d'. It would appear that for the faster event rates of twelve and twenty-four events per minute, the event rate was more important than the signal probability in determining the detectability of the signal, since the difference in d' between signal rates at either of these two event rates was much smaller than the difference in d' between the event rates. At the slowest event rate of six events per minute, d' was higher with the faster auditory signal rate, but lower with the faster visual signal rate (see Figure 10).

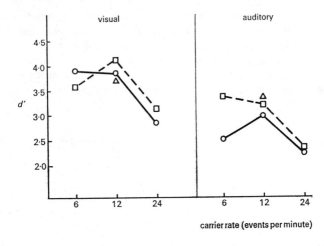

Figure 10 The detectability (d') of signals in relation to signal rate and carrier (event) rate (Loeb and Binford, 1968)

Motivation

The cost of an observing response and the reward for a detection can be varied by altering the rewards and cost attached to the different outcomes. Such changes may also affect the criterion, and it is not always possible to determine whether the first or second decision level is being affected. It is probable that any form of knowledge of results or punishment that is contingent upon correct detections or misses will increase the observing responses, but they may also lead to a more relaxed criterion. Punishment for false alarms will lead to a stricter criterion, but may also increase the level of arousal. Jerison (1967c) has described an experiment demonstrating the effect of changing the level of punishment for omissions. A monkey was trained to respond to a signal by pressing a lever. The signal was a flashing light, and if there was no response within eight seconds, the monkey received a moderate shock. When the shock was increased, the monkey ceased to pay attention to the display. Instead, he hit the lever once a second, thus insuring that he would never receive a shock. These regular responses Jerison called 'free responses'. When the cost of 'free responses' was increased by giving a weak shock when the lever was pressed in the absence of a signal, the animal vacillated between making 'free responses' and attending to the display. With a further increase in the lever shock, the animal reverted to his attentive strategy, and emitted almost no 'free responses'. The cost (shock) of the free responses now outweighed the cost of an occasional missed signal.

Levine (1966) varied the costs of missed signals and false alarms, in monetary values. The number of false alarms was very low, even for those subjects with high costs for misses and no cost for false alarms. False alarms increased as the cost of a miss increased, and decreased as the cost of a false alarm increased, as would be expected. *Beta*, however, increased with both kinds of increased cost. There seems to be evidence that the number of false alarms is related to the number of signals that subjects expect.

Summary and Conclusions

It is clear that the *event rate* is an important factor in determining the level of detections in a vigilance task. The importance of the event rate is one of the main reasons for the suggestion that the vigilance decrement is due to habituation, since the rate of habituation is dependent on the event rate. It is probable that the occurrence of a signal reverses habituation to some extent, and therefore it is to be exptected that there would be a relationship between the level of performance and the probability that an event will be a signal. This probability is not, however, the whole story, and two experiments have shown that the event rate may be more important than the signal rate.

It has been suggested that there are two processes of decision in a vigilance task. The first process involves the decision to observe or pay attention to the display and the second involves the decision to give a positive response to a particular event. The decision to make an observation may depend on the cost of such an observation. The cost per unit time increases as the event rate increases, and the cost per event may also increase, due to habituation. The automatic inhibition of the neural response to such an observation of a repeated event may be regarded as making it more difficult to pay attention to that event. Periods of non-observation of the display may result in an increase in the neural response. Such periods of non-observation may involve moments of drowsiness. It is, however, possible to discuss the decrement in performance in terms of the neural changes without involving the more tenuous concept of the observing response. It should also be noticed that the event rate affects the expectancy or ability of the subject to predict a signal.

5 Expectancy and Preparatory Set

Detection Probability and Reaction Time

Temporal Expectancy: Signal Rate and Signal Interval

In the section of his discussion entitled 'Expectancy', N. H. Mackworth (1950) suggested that fluctuations in the minute-by-minute accuracy of the subject were due to changes in his attitude or set. He quoted Mowrer (1940) who showed that when subjects had been trained to react to a sequence of tones occurring at twelve-second intervals, their reactions to a tone following a different interval were slower. Both Mowrer and Mackworth found that readiness to react was lowest following the shortest interval.

Any increase in the uncertainty of a signal will have a considerable effect on the ability of the subject to detect that signal. Egan *et al.* (1961a) showed that when the interval of time uncertainty was increased from zero to eight seconds, there was a considerable decrease in the detectability of the signal, as measured by d' (see chapter 2). Most of this decrease took place as the interval was increased from zero to two seconds. Egan *et al.* (1961b) used a light to indicate that a signal had or would occur. Maximum detectability was found when the signal occurred 0·25 seconds after the onset of the light. (See also Klemmer, 1956).

Deese (1955) put forward the suggestion that the basic decrement in a vigilance task was due to the disappearance of an initial excitatory state, as a result of the reduced sensory input. Within this basic hypothesis of changes in arousal, he emphasized the importance of expectancy as a determinant of the probability of detection of a particular signal. The level of expectancy is determined by the actual course of stimulus events during previous experience with the task. In addition to an overall level of expectancy determined by past events, there will be short-range fluctuations dependent on immediate events. Expectancy should be low immediately following a signal, should increase as the mean intersignal interval is approached, and continue to increase as the intersignal interval increases. Deese added that the observer's extrapolation of the future behaviour of the search field is separate from his vigilance for the signals in that field. His vigilance level may depend on such factors as motivation and physiological arousal as well as on the past series of signals. He pointed out that it was probable that observers maintained too high a criterion for admitting that a signal had occurred. His outline of the processes underlying the vigilance decrement covered most of the areas which have later been filled in by various authors.

There is considerable evidence in favour of the expectancy hypothesis. It rests upon three main findings:

1. The effect of signal probability. This includes changes in signal rate and changes in the event rate and is considered under three aspects: the effect of signal rate within a session, the effect of signal rate in a training session on performance in a test session, and the event rate (see chapter 3).

2. The effect of variability of signal interval, and the relation between the length of the preceding interval and performance on a particular signal.

3. The ability of the subject to estimate the mean interval.

It should be emphasized that Deese (1955) regarded expectancy as tending to maintain vigilance against a background of deterioration in alertness due to the monotonous environment. In various active tasks (see J. F. Mackworth, 1969) which show a decrement in performance, the subject is often highly trained so that his expectancy as to the probable nature of the next event is unlikely to change during a session. In such a case, the basic decrement almost certainly depends on the monotonous nature of the incoming stimuli. In a vigilance task, the subject may decide that it is safe for him to relax his attention immediately following a signal. This short rest pause may help to maintain the level of alertness or to reduce the habituation of the neural response to the events.

The recent finding that there is a decrease in both detections and false alarms during a session can be interpreted either on the assumption that there is a change in the expectancy of the subject, or that there is a reduction in the neural response to the events of the task (see chapter 2). It would, however, seem that changes in the apparent probability of the signal should lead to changes in the detectability of the signal, and such changes are seldom found. A more satisfactory description of behaviour may be found in the suggestion that changes in signal probability affect the decision to make an observation of the display (see chapter 3).

Signal Probability

Signal rate

In general, increasing the signal rate improves performance. A higher signal rate should both increase the level of arousal, or reduce the rate of habituation, and also increase the ability of the subject to predict when a signal will occur.

The probability of detection of signals in a radar display with temporal and spatial uncertainty was reduced as the number of signals per hour was reduced from forty to ten per hour (Deese, 1955). Jenkins (1958) reported that the percentage of detections of an increased deviation of a meter pointer was reduced as the signal rate was reduced from 480 to 7·5 per hour. He also found that the rate of decrement of detections was faster when the signal rate was lower (see Figure 11). The probability of a false alarm was highest with the high signal rate, but even so, the data suggested that the actual detectability of the signal was higher than the high signal rate. McDonald and Burns (1964) used signal rates of 60 and 12 per hour and found that over-all probability of detection was higher with the faster signal rate, but there was no difference in the rate of decrement between the two signal frequencies.

Two proof-reading tasks also showed a higher probability of detection of errors when there were more errors. Kappauf

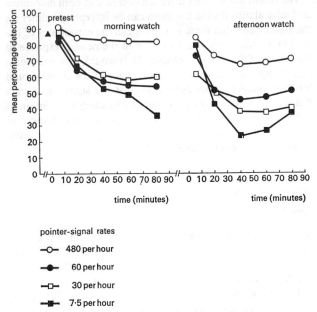

Figure 11 Effect of signal rate on detection (Jenkins, 1958)

and Powe (1959) used an audio-visual checking task, and found maximum decrement with the slowest error rate of eight per hour, and least decrement with the fastest rate of eighty per hour. Ellis and Ahr (1960) found an improvement in probability of error detection as the error rate increased from six to thirty errors in 1555 words, but with sixty and 120 errors there was a slight decrease in probability of detection.

Colquhoun (1961) compared the detection of seventy-two

and twelve signals in forty minutes in a situation in which there were either 144 or twenty-four events (strips of six discs) in the forty minutes. He found maximum probability of detection with seventy-two signals; the lowest probability of detection was found with twelve signals in 144 events, though no decrement was found in this condition during the session. Thus the difference between the conditions was maximal at the beginning of the session. When the event rate was decreased to twenty-four events, of which half were signals, the probability of detection of the twelve signals was the same as that found with seventy-two signals in 144 events (see Figure 7, p. 68). He therefore suggested that the probability of detection was determined by the probability that an event would be a signal, rather than by the absolute probability of a signal in a certain time interval. This is not always the case, as shown by Jerison (1967c) and Loeb and Binford (1968) (see chapter 4, Figure 10).

Latency of response. Bowen (1964) presented a simulated radar test in which the signal was a spot of light that flashed until it was seen. When only one signal was presented in an hour, the detection of this signal took longer at the end of the hour than it did at the beginning, and at the end of the hour it took longer to detect than the signals that had been presented at rates of ten or twenty per hour.

The effect of signal rate and variability of signal interval on latency of response to a light was examined by Bevan *et al.* (1965). The latency increased as the signal rate decreased from six per minute to twenty-two per hour, but there was no further increase in latency with the slowest signal rate of ten per hour. In each case the latency was longer for the variable than for the regular interval. It was found that the response latency stabilized at the fourth trial in a series.

A similar experiment on visual latency was reported by R. P. Smith *et al.* (1966). Two lights flashed alternately, and the signal was an occasional flash of the wrong light. The signal rates were six, twenty-four or ninety-six per hour. The variability of the signal interval was also given at three levels. The latency of response was inversely related to the signal density, but the interval variability only had an effect with the lowest signal rate.

Johnston *et al.* (1966) varied the signal rate and the visual load independently. There were either four, eight, sixteen or thirty-two visual combinations of digits and letters appearing simultaneously, and the signal was a change in the number of stimuli, either an extra one or a disappearance. There were sixty or 100 signals in a 100-minute session. Latencies were longer and a higher percentage of signals was omitted with fewer signals. Longest latencies were found with the high stimulus density and the low signal rate. With the low signal rate, latencies were shortest at the mean intersignal intervals of 90–100 seconds and showed considerable increases on either side of this mean interval.

An auditory vigilance task was studied by Martz (1966), who presented trains of twelve successive tones, each one 2dB above the previous one. There were three seconds between each tone. The train constituted a signal, and the subject responded as soon as he heard a tone. The signal rates were one, 2·5, 7·5 and 15 per hour. Signals were reported at a lower intensity when they occurred more often. There was a significant increase in the intensity required for detection with the lower signal rates when the first hour was compared with the pretest, but this was not found with the two higher rates. There were no significant changes within the watch. A further experiment (Martz, 1967) showed that latencies increased during the watch with the lowest signal rate of two signals in forty-eight minutes. Performance improved with increasing rate up to fifteen signals per hour.

Artificial signals. In a field situation, the rate and variability of the real events which must be detected are not under control. It is, however, possible to add other signals to such tasks and to give information to the subjects as to their performance on these extra signals. Therefore, many experiments have studied

the effect of adding extra signals on the detection of a particular set of signals. When the 'artificial' signals are not distinguishable from the real ones, this represents a simple increase
in signal rate, unless knowledge of results is added. If the
extra signals are distinguishable from the real ones and in fact
temporally independent of them, then the extra signals may be
acting only as an arousing or dishabituating stimulus.

Garvey *et al.* (1959) showed that the addition of artificial
signals improved performance on the real ones, whether they
were the same or different from the real ones. The real signal
was a deflection of a dial pointer into a marked area, and the
artificial signal was either the same or a deflection in the
opposite direction. No decrement occurred during the session
when the artificial signals were added; when loud noises or
warning lights were added to the artificial signals, performance
on the real signals was improved even further.

The effect of extra signals on a dial-reading task was also
examined by Faulkner (1962). The subjects were tested for
three periods of twenty-seven minutes each, with a five-
minute rest between periods. In one period there were nine
signals, and in the other two there were thirty-six. In one of the
thirty-six signal periods the intersignal interval range was
large, 10–110 seconds, while in the other it was small, 50–70
seconds. It was found that latency was greatest for the period
with nine signals, and least for the period with a small range
of intersignal intervals. There was an increase in latency between the first and third periods.

The addition of *knowledge of results* to the extra or artificial
signals is a valuable way of maintaining performance. Mc-
Cormack and colleagues found that knowledge of results on
30 per cent of the signals was adequate to maintain the speed
of response (McCormack *et al.*, 1963; McCormack and Mc-
Elheran, 1963). Two extra signals were added by C. H. Baker
(1960b) in the longer intervals of the original Mackworth
series. Knowledge of results given on these two extra signals in
each half hour greatly improved detection of the other signals.
Wilkinson (1964) found that the addition of an extra forty

signals to eight original signals per hour did not improve detection, but when knowledge of results was given on the extra signals, there was a considerable improvement in detection of the original signals.

Two kinds of signals. When two kinds of signals are given, the resultant division of attention may be more harmful than any advantage due to the extra signals (see chapter 3). Binford and Loeb (1963) found that the addition of auditory signals to a visual vigilance task *increased* the latency of response to the visual signals. With a further increase in the number of auditory signals, the latency of response decreased, and the probability of detection of the visual signals increased. They interpreted these data as indicating that apart from the effect of division of attention, the extra auditory signals increased arousal. It is clear that the effect of extra signals is not only due to an increase in the predictability of the signals (see Figure 12).

Previous experience

The theory of expectancy would predict that the previous experience of the subject should have a considerable effect on his performance. Wiener (1963) trained subjects with one of three signal rates: sixteen, thirty-two, or forty-eight signals in forty-eight minutes. On the second day, all the subjects received thirty-two signals. The group trained with forty-eight signals detected most, and the group trained with sixteen detected fewest signals in the test session. The sixteen-signal group also gave fewest false responses. A similar finding was reported by Colquhoun and Baddeley (1964, 1967). Subjects were trained with high or low rates of signals, and tested on high or low rates. Subjects trained at the low rate detected fewer signals and gave fewer false alarms than those trained on the high signal rate, especially at the beginning of the test period (see Figure 13). Significant decrements in detections during the test session were found only with those subjects who had been trained on the high signal rate. There was no

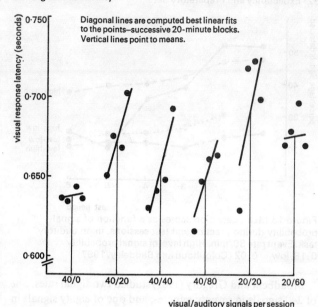

Figure 12 Means of median latencies of response to visual signals (Binford and Loeb, 1963)

difference in the detectability of the signals for the different groups, as measured by d', but there were significant differences in *beta*, a measure of the criterial level adopted by the subjects. *Beta* was higher with those subjects who had been trained with the low signal rate, indicating that these subjects were less ready to make a positive response than those trained with the high signal rate. There was a significant increase in *beta* during the test session for those subjects who had been trained with the high rate and tested with the low rate. This finding gives support to the suggestion that the vigilance decrement is due to a change in criterion as the subject finds that there are fewer signals than he was expecting (see chapter 2).

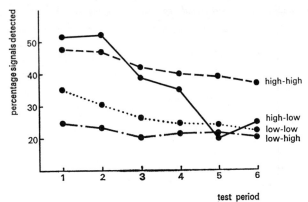

Figure 13 Mean detection scores as a function of signal probability during practice and test sessions, in an auditory task. Event rate 30/min. High level of signal probability = 0·18, low = 0·02 (Colquhoun and Baddeley, 1967)

Broadbent and Gregory (1965) studied two signal rates, one of 240 signals in seventy minutes, and one of eighty signals in seventy minutes. The subjects were practised on the same signal rate as that with which they were tested. Fewer false alarms were given with the low signal rate, and the value for *beta* was higher, indicating that the subjects were adopting a more strict criterion. In the first day's testing with the low signal rate, this criterial measure became higher during the session indicating an increase in caution, but on the second day the change was in the opposite direction.

These then are the positive data relating to signal rate. There is considerable evidence that an increase in signal rate will improve detection and the readiness to respond to a signal. This effect is predicted by both the expectancy theory and the arousal or habituation theory. There are also a number of experiments in which no effect of signal rate has been found.

Negative results. Signal rates of thirty or twelve per hour were presented in alternate hours of an auditory vigilance task lasting for nine hours (Webb and Wherry, 1960). In another experiment there were twelve sessions of visual and auditory tasks with six signals per hour and eight sessions with thirty signals per hour (Buckner *et al.*, 1965). No differences in detections due to signal rate were found. Bergum and Lehr (1962a and b, 1963a) tested rates of six and twenty-four signals per hour and found a significant difference in only one of many experiments.

J. F. Mackworth (1963a) presented signals on alternating black and white segments of a clock face and found that a higher percentage of signals was detected when there were only twenty-four signals on the black segments than when there were also twenty-four signals on the white segments, a total of forty-eight signals per hour. J. F. Mackworth (1968) compared signal rates of thirty and 180 per hour on two kinds of clock task, and found that there was no difference in the percentage detected, but more false alarms were given with the low signal rate, suggesting that subjects were expecting more signals than there actually were.

In a task in which the signal was a change in one of twelve simultaneous displays, the latency of response was slightly longer when there were sixteen signals than when there were sixty-four, but this difference was not significant (Montague *et al.*, 1965). Davies and Hockey (1966) studied a digit-checking task, with two rates of discrepancies, forty-five and ninety signals per hour, and found no main effects of signal frequency. It can be concluded that while signal rate may affect the readiness to detect and respond to a signal, better performance being found with higher signal rates, this is not always the case.

Signal Interval

The expectancy theory suggests that a subject's performance depends on his ability to predict the occurrence of a signal. As a result of his estimation of the probability of a signal, he will pay attention to the display (make an observing response,

see chapter 3). He assesses this probability from his past experience in a complex way. His first judgement may be on the
basis of whether or not any recognizable pattern may be expected. In many practical situations quite different frequencies may be expected at different times. For instance, a driver
will expect a great many more hazards and decisions when
driving through a busy town than when driving along a free-
way. In most experimental situations, the subject will assume
that the experimenter has imposed some restrictions upon a
completely random sequence of events, and the subject will
regard part of his task to involve guessing these restrictions, so
that he can pay attention only at those times when a signal is
to be expected. It appears to be very difficult for anyone to
remain continuously alert in a monotonous task.

The simplest hypothesis that a subject can evolve from a
series of very irregular intervals is that there are unlikely to be
any very short intervals. He will then tend to relax his attention immediately after seeing a signal, and pay more attention
as the interval lengthens. This is the basic expectancy hypothesis, which suggests that the *probability of detection of a
signal is least when the intersignal interval is shortest* (Deese,
1955). N. H. Mackworth (1950) pointed out that the signals
with the lowest probability of detection in the clock test were
those following intervals of 0·75 to 1 minute. He suggested
that this was due to the fact that the instructions and the test
as a whole led the subject to believe that signal intervals
would be fairly long, so that subjects relaxed their vigilance
after a signal.

Deese (1955) further suggested that the subject was probably carrying out a continuous averaging process, so that his
expectancy was constructed not merely from the temporal
location of the previous signal, but from the whole series of
intervals that he had received. The subject was able to form an
idea of the average rate of signal presentation and act on this.
C. H. Baker (1959b) enlarged this idea by suggesting that
temporal expectancy would be at a maximum around the
mean intersignal interval and would fall off on either side of

the mean. He also pointed out that the ability of the observer to perform this averaging process must depend not only on the mean intersignal interval but also on the variability of the signal interval.

Most of the experiments concerned directly with the variability of the signal interval have employed reaction time tasks. When a signal is not reported, it is difficult to assess the effective intersignal interval. This has been discussed in detail by McGrath and Harabedian (1963). They compared two distributions of signal intervals. One was rectangular and the other was skewed. Nearly half the signal intervals were less than one minute in the latter condition. The mean signal interval was 2–2·5 minutes. With the rectangular distribution of intervals, from 9–300 seconds, there was an increase in the probability of detection as the preceding interval increased. This was true whether the interval was measured from the last signal presented, or from the last signal detected. With the skewed distribution of intervals, in which the short intervals were highly probable, there was no relation between the probability of detection of a signal and the interval between it and the previous presented signal. The data from those subjects who had *detected* the previous signal showed a *decrease* in detection as the interval increased, but when these data from the skewed distribution were analysed in terms of the subjects who had *missed* the previous signal, there was an *increasing* probability of detection with an increasing interval, as found with the rectangular distribution. The data would suggest that some subjects recognized the skewed signal distribution while others did not.

A fairly regular series of intersignal intervals will have several advantages for a subject. It allows him to learn the probable interval, so that his performance may improve during a session. He can learn to pay attention at the right moment, which increases his ability to detect the signal, and in between these times he can relax, so that he does not exhaust his ability to pay attention. It increases the number of signals that he detects in a detection task, so that the reward or dishabituating effect of the signals is maximal. Thus, accurate expectancy can prevent the occurrence of the decrement, though it cannot therefore be concluded that changes in expectancy are the cause of the decrement. Deese (1955) pointed out that the decrement was due to the monotonous sensory background to the vigilance task. Within this situation the vigilance of the observer will vary from moment to moment according to assessment of the probability of a signal (N. H. Mackworth, 1950). This assessment will be least accurate when the variability of the intersignal intervals is greatest. C. H. Baker (1959a and b) examined a radar task in which twenty-four signals per hour were given. The variability of the intersignal interval ranged from zero (completely regular) through medium (1–6 minutes) to irregular (0·75–10 minutes, the original Mackworth times). He found that with the regular and medium irregularity, no decrement in detection occurred during the session. The best over-all performance was found with the regular series. A significant decrement during the session was only found with the most irregular series.

Other workers have examined the effect of signal regularity upon reaction times. Dardano (1965) examined three levels of intersignal variability and found that reaction time (R T) was shortest with the minimum variability. In the medium variability condition, the longest R T was found with those signals that followed the shortest intersignal interval. There was no relation between intersignal interval and R T for the session with the greatest intersignal interval variability. Three levels of variability were also examined by McCormack and Prysiazniuk (1961). These were either regular, 30–90 or 10–110 seconds. The shortest mean R T was found with the regular interval and the longest with the most irregular. There was, however, no significant interaction between conditions and time periods. All groups showed increases in reaction time over periods that were effectively parallel.

A similar result was found by Boulter and Adams (1963) in a reaction time task. They also employed three levels of signal uncertainty, ranging from completely regular intervals of 220 seconds to 15–900 seconds for the high uncertainty. There were no significant differences between conditions or between the rates of increase of R T during the sessions with the three conditions. Decrements in speed of response were found with all conditions. They found that there was a marked difference between the medium and high uncertainty conditions in the relation between reaction time and signal interval. With the medium variability, R T was longest with the shortest interval of 120 seconds, while with the high uncertainty, R T was minimal with the shortest intervals of fifteen seconds, and increased as the interval increased. These data suggest that the medium variability allowed the subject to form an estimate of the probability of a signal, while with the high uncertainty he could not do so. In this case, it is possible that the arousal or dishabituating effect of one signal would be more likely to affect the response to the next when the interval between them was short. Although there were no significant differences between the changes over time, the medium uncertainty curve showed least change over time, suggesting that some of the subjects might have been learning the interval probability.

Expectancies are built up not only during a session, but also before it, as suggested by N. H. Mackworth (1950). Therefore, the previous experience of the subject may be of importance, as demonstrated by Colquhoun and Baddeley (1964, 1967). C. H. Baker (1959a) used subjects who had taken part in previous experiments with the medium level of variability. McCormack and Prysiazniuk (1961) tested all subjects with all three levels. Boulter and Adams (1963) trained their subjects on the same range of intervals that they received in the test. Thus it seems that there should have been no change in expectancy during the session, and the increase in latency found during the session should be unrelated to any change in expectancy.

The relation between the preceding interval and performance on a particular signal has been discussed by a number of other authors, N. H. Mackworth (1950) found that with the listening test and the Clock Test, detection was least efficient with signals immediately following the very short intervals, and most signals were detected when they followed the longest intervals of 5–10 minutes. On the other hand, the radar test showed that the lowest percentage of signals was detected when they followed the long intervals, with the best performance following the medium intervals of two minutes. Mackworth suggested that this difference was due to *spatial expectancy*. There was some possibility of predicting where the next signal would occur on the radar screen, since the same order of positions was repeated each half-hour. The comparative effects of spatial and temporal uncertainty were also examined by Adams and Boulter (1964). Spatial uncertainty had a greater effect on reaction time than did temporal uncertainty, but a reliable increase in R T during the session was found only with temporal uncertainty.

With an interval ranging from 30 seconds to 90, McCormack *et al.* (1962) found that reaction time was longest following a thirty-second interval, and decreased to a minimum at seventy-five seconds. When knowledge of results was supplied, the reaction time was minimal at the mean interval of sixty seconds.

Estimation of the Mean Interval

The first postulate of the expectancy theory is that expectancy for a signal will be lowest immediately following a signal and will gradually rise. This is similar to the scallop-shaped response rates found in operant conditioning experiments when the animal is working on a fixed-interval schedule (Skinner, 1938). The second postulate is that subjects can estimate the mean of an irregular series, and that their reactivity will be maximal at the mean interval and again fall off as the mean is exceeded. Several authors have demonstrated that subjects readily form estimates about signal intervals when presented with a series. Mowrer (1940) presented tones at intervals of twelve seconds. Occasionally a tone was inserted at a different interval, ranging from three to twenty-four seconds. The reaction time to the unexpected signal was longest following the very brief interval, and became shorter as the interval approached the standard. As the interval increased beyond the standard, there was again an increase in the reaction time.

This experiment was repeated by C. H. Baker (1959b) who presented one unexpected interval following a series of twenty intervals of ten seconds each. The final interval varied from two to thirty seconds. He found the same results as Mowrer. C. H. Baker (1962a) presented a series of signals with varying intervals and asked the subject to generate the next two intervals in the series, which lasted for twenty to thirty minutes. Two different ranges of variability were used, the Mackworth intervals, 0·75 to ten minutes, and a range of 1·5 to 4·5 minutes. Two other programmes of signals were used, in which the intervals were two-thirds of those described. The measure was the duration of the subject-generated intervals. The mean lengths of these intervals were remarkably close to the mean of the series. The standard deviation was greater with the greater range of intervals. Since the expectancy theory states that the subject averages over a large number of previous intervals, the product-moment coefficient between the length of the generated interval and previous intervals was calculated. While only one coefficient was significantly different from zero, the coefficients were predominantly positive up to six or seven intervals back in the series.

This series of experiments was continued by C. H. Baker (1962b) with one in which subjects were presented with signals on the Continuous Clock at intervals varying from 0·5 to 7·5 minutes. Subjects were told when they had missed a signal. After eight signals presented at a mean rate of one in four minutes, a ninth was presented at an interval varying from 0·25 to ten minutes. It was found that the probability that this final signal would be detected was significantly lower when it followed the interval of ten minutes than when it followed a shorter interval. When only those subjects whose performance fell in the middle range were considered, there was also a drop for the very short interval of 0·25 minutes.

Three adaptation series were used by Hardesty and Bevan (1965) with intervals of ten, twenty or forty seconds, followed by a test series with intervals of five to eighty seconds. It was found that in each case the minimal reaction time occurred with the same interval as that presented in the adaptation series. In a second experiment, the adaptation series was variable, with ranges from 50 per cent less to 50 per cent greater than the average. The reaction times to the test series were closely similar to those obtained with the regular intervals. Finally, they presented a series in which the mean (ten seconds), mode (fifteen seconds), and midrange (twenty seconds) were different. There was a skewed distribution, such that 50 per cent of the signals occurred after the shortest intervals of ten seconds. The lowest reaction time to the test series was found after the mean interval. This result was different from that found by McGrath and Harabedian (1963), which might have been due to the fact that much shorter intervals were used by Hardesty and Bevan. These authors suggested that a mechanism similar to the adaptation level in sensory judgements determines response latencies.

In a further experiment, Bevan, Avant and Lankford (1966) varied the distribution of intervals around twenty seconds, followed by a test interval. Reaction time was maximal following the shorter intervals and minimal for the mean interval both during the series and also in the final test.

It can be concluded that subjects can and do vary their state of vigilance or readiness to detect and respond to a signal, according to their estimate of the temporal probability of a signal. It would seem, however, that this ability would act to prevent the decrement rather than to cause it.

Spatial Uncertainty

N. H. Mackworth (1950) found that the relation between signal interval and probability of detection was different for the Clock Test and the Radar Test, and he suggested that this was related to the fact that spatial uncertainty was maximal for the Clock Test but somewhat less for the Radar Test. The effect of spatial uncertainty was examined by Adams and Boulter (1962). In the first experiment, there were four visual sources of a signal, which was the appearance of a two-digit number. A cue light appeared above one of the four sources at two-second intervals. In the repetitive condition, this light appeared in sequence across the four sources, while in the unsystematic condition it appeared in a random distribution. Subjects were told to follow the cue light, since a signal would appear at a source when that cue light was on. It was found that the latency was longer with the unsystematic condition, but there was no significant difference in the rate of increase in latency during the session with the two conditions. The speed of response was almost twice as fast with the unsystematic cue light as it was in another experiment with no cue light. It was found that with the repetitive cues, responses to all sources were equal; with the unsystematic condition, responses to the central sources were as fast as with the repetitive condition, but responses to the outer sources were much slower.

The relation between temporal and spatial uncertainty was further examined by Adams and Boulter (1964). There were three signal sources. With spatial certainty, the signals moved from one source to the next systematically. There were nine signals in each half-hour. Mean response latency increased as uncertainty increased, being minimal for both spatial and temporal certainty, and maximal with both kinds of uncertainty. Temporal uncertainty was better than spatial uncertainty alone. However, only temporal uncertainty showed a significant decrement. These data would suggest that while spatial uncertainty is a powerful factor in the speed of response, the knowledge of *when* a signal will occur is even more important in relation to the decrement during a session. The search requirement may act as a dishabituating factor, while the knowledge of the temporal pattern may allow the subject to take short rests (see Figure 14).

A comparison of the effects of spatial and temporal

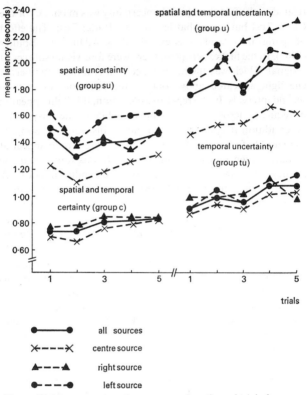

Figure 14 Mean response latency as a function of trials for each of four groups (Adams and Boulter, 1964)

uncertainty was reported by Kulp and Alluisi (1967). Two, four, eight, or sixteen lights were used as signal sources. In the choice reaction task, a buzzer sounded two seconds before the signal, and signals were presented at a rate of four a minute. In the watchkeeping task, with temporal uncertainty, signals were presented twenty-four times an hour. No analysis of change over time was presented. It was found that response time increased as the spatial uncertainty increased, and that the rate of increase between conditions was maximal with one version of the watchkeeping task, in which there was low compatibility between stimulus and response spatial arrangements. With high compatibility, and only two lights, there was very little difference between the watchkeeping performance and the choice-reaction performance. The signal light

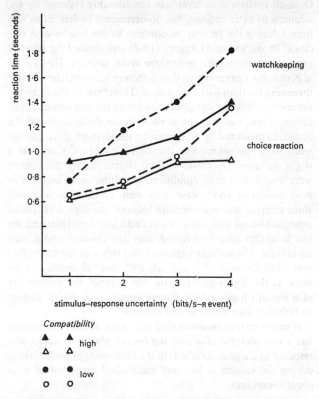

Figure 15 Reaction time in a visual vigilance task as a function of stimulus–response uncertainty. In the watchkeeping task, signal rate = 24/hr. Choice reaction task, signal rate = 4/min. Two to sixteen lights as signal sources (Kulp and Alluisi, 1967)

was brief but well above threshold. It was concluded that the contributions of different sources of uncertainty were linearly additive (see Figure 15).

The effect of the number of signal sources was examined in a signal detection task by Jerison (1963). He compared detection with one, two or three clocks on which the signal might appear. Over-all performance level was considerably reduced by the addition of extra sources, but no decrement in detections was found during the session, in contrast to the results with one clock. Broadbent and Gregory (1965) also studied the effect of presenting signals on one or three visual sources. They found in preliminary experiments that detection was much lower with three sources than with one source. Therefore, in the main experiment a brighter signal was used with the three-source condition. There was a slight increase in the detectability of the signal, as measured by d', during the session with three sources while with one source and the same signal rate, there was a slight decrease. Decreases in false alarms during the session were found with both conditions, resulting in an increase in *beta*, indicating an increase in caution. The level of *beta* with three sources was intermediate between the high level (strict criterion) found with one channel and a low signal rate and the low level (lax criterion) found with one channel and a high signal rate. The authors suggested that this was due to the fact that while the over-all signal rate with three channels was the same as the high signal rate on one channel, the probability of a signal on one of the three channels was similar to that with the low signal rate on one channel.

It can therefore be concluded that while spatial uncertainty has a considerable effect on the overall ability to detect and respond to a signal, its effect on the decrement of performance during the session is less well established than that of temporal uncertainty.

Neurophysiological Concomitants of Expectancy

Walter (1964a and b) and colleagues (Walter *et al.*, 1964) studied the evoked potentials appearing over the scalp in different regions when a repetitive stimulus was given, and when this stimulus was paired with a second stimulus to which a response was required. When stimuli are given in any modality, evoked potentials can be recorded over wide areas of the frontal cortex. Habituation of these non-specific responses is rapid; when, however, the repeated stimulus is coupled with a second, to which a response is required, the cortical response to the first stimulus is augmented, while the evoked potential response to the second signal stimulus declines with repetition. In this situation, the secondary surface-negative response to the first stimulus is prolonged until the second stimulus occurs. This prolonged response preceding an expected signal was termed the Contingent Negative Variation (CNV) because it arose when a second stimulus was contingent on the first.

Walter (1964a) suggested that the brain responses reflect a probabilistic analysis of the stimulus situation in terms of information content. In other words, the brain constructs expectancies about the nature of the immediate future from past data (see J. F. Mackworth, 1969). While habituation is the result of a repeated stimulus that matches the model and is not a signal for action, contingent amplification results from increasing probability of association, where the first stimulus indicates that the second will require a response. The CNV was also named the Expectancy or E-wave. The development of the E-wave is accompanied by reduced reaction time. Within subjects, the fastest reaction times have the largest E-waves (Wasak and Obrist, 1969). It is very sensitive to social influences, being evoked by a word or movement by the experimenter. If the subject is told that the conditional stimulus will not be followed by the second unconditional one, the E-wave immediately disappears. If, however, the second stimulus unexpectedly fails to follow the first, the E-wave appears, and disappears at the exact moment that the second stimulus should have occurred. If the second stimulus continues to be absent, the E–wave gradually disappears, and even if the second stimulus is restored, the E–wave never again reaches its former height. There is always some residual uncertainty. In general, the E–wave does not appear unless the probability that a second stimulus will appear is greater than 0·5.

The E–wave follows cessation of a continuous stimulus and is not proportional to the energy of the stimulus. In normal adults it is the most constant and predictable electrocortical feature. It has also been found that when a subject is asked to estimate a temporal interval, and make a response after two seconds, the E–wave occupies the interval.

Walter (1964b) pointed out that responses in the nonspecific frontal cortex are extremely sensitive to distraction, boredom and drowsiness. There is a considerable gap between this promising research and vigilance tasks. However, the E–wave is sensitive to many of the features that are significant in vigilance, and future research may show that the two sets of findings are related.

Summary and Conclusions

The ability of a subject to predict when and where a signal will occur has a marked effect on his ability to detect and respond to that signal. In a vigilance task the predictability of the signal is normally very small – usually less than 1 per cent of the events in a task are signals. Anything that improves the ability to predict will therefore improve performance. A higher frequency of signals and a lower event rate will both help. A reduced variability of signal interval may also be effective. In the usual vigilance task, however, the only estimate of signal probability that the subject can make is that there is unlikely to be a signal within a certain period of time after the last one. This may result in poorer performance on the signal that follows a previous one after an unusually short interval. Training the subject with the signal rate that he will receive in the test is helpful. In a practical situation, however, the only change that can be made, apart from increasing the detectability of the signal, may be the addition of artificial signals, on which knowledge of results can be given.

It is clear that there are two kinds of expectation developed in a vigilance task. There is the expectancy that a particular event will be a signal, and there is the expectancy that a particular event will not be a signal. These two attitudes are interdependent, but since the probability of a non-signal event so greatly outweighs the probability of a signal, the vigilance decrement may arise from the reinforcing of this second aspect of the situation as it unfolds to the subject. The concept of habituation is linked to the concept that the organism learns to expect a stimulus to which he need not respond. From this concept arises the idea of a neural model (see J. F. Mackworth, 1968b, 1969).

Because there is such a high probability that an event will not be a signal, the neural and physiological responses to the event are inhibited. There will be a decrease in positive responses, both correct and incorrect, leading to an apparent change in the criterion of the subject. This may even be accompanied by an apparent increase in the detectability of the signal, as the apparent intensity of the events is decreased (see chapter 2).

The rise in *beta*, representing a more strict criterion, that occurs during a vigilance task, may be due to a change in expectancy during the task. The criterial level may, however, stabilize in later sessions (Binford and Loeb, 1966; Broadbent and Gregory, 1965), although decrements in detections and increases in reaction times have been found after many sessions (see chapter 7). It is therefore doubtful whether the decrement can be entirely due to changes in expectancy. There may also be an element of change in arousal level. More active tasks such as tracking show decrements in performance even though there can be no change in expectancy. Such inhibition resulting from a repeated series of stimuli would seem to indicate that the mechanism for paying attention to the novel or unexpected stimulus is separate from the mechanism for paying attention to the expected stimulus.

6 Knowledge of Results and Motivation

Knowledge of results (K R) is essential for improvement to occur in most activities. This feedback is often supplied by a direct comparison of actual with required performance. In tracking tasks, a subject can see for himself how accurately his pointer follows the target. In tennis, a player sees the difference between where he put the ball and where he would like to have put it. In the average vigilance task, however, the observer receives no information at all about his responses. In general there is little evidence that learning occurs from one session to another in a visual vigilance task, though there is often found to be improvement from one session to the next in an auditory task (see chapter 7). Feedback has two main effects in a vigilance task. It may enable the subject to learn something about the signal, and it may have a motivating or activating effect. It is difficult to separate these two factors, but a number of experiments have contributed evidence which helps to disentangle them.

In tracking and other tasks, the interacting factors of fatigue and learning can be separated by examining the differences between performance at the end of one session and the beginning of the next. It is assumed that performance at the beginning of the second session indicates the level of performance that would have been reached at the end of the first if fatigue had not depressed the level. A similar interaction is to be expected in the vigilance task. If K R is producing learning, then the addition of K R should show an increasing difference between control and K R conditions as the session continues, and also in a following session there should be a difference between the two groups when they are both tested under control conditions.

Performance in a later session may depend on the kind of K R that was given. Subjects who were told only that they had missed a signal might be expected to increase their false alarms, since the cost of missed signals would now be increased as compared with the cost of a false alarm. This aspect has not been widely explored as yet.

Detections

N. H. Mackworth (1950) examined the effect of K R on the detection of signals on the Jump Clock, and in the Listening Test. Full K R was given over a loudspeaker by the experimenter, who commented on detections, missed signals and false alarms. The data showed that when K R was given, detection was definitely better, and there was little or no decrement in detection during the session. It was also found that there was an interaction between the effect of K R and the order of sessions. Subjects who received K R in the first session were only slightly worse without K R in the second session. But subjects who had the control session first were definitely better in the second session with K R. Subjects who received the control condition in two sessions detected considerably fewer signals in the second session than in the first. These data could be explained on the assumption that K R in the first session resulted in a better performance in the second control session than would have been found if the first session had also been without K R. The results suggested that the subjects had learned something about the task from the first K R session that enabled them to perform better in the second session.

Pollack and Knaff (1958) examined the detection of an increased deflection of the needle of a meter. In the K R condition, a horn blared when a signal was missed. Other variables were the ambient lighting and reward at the end of the session. The horn improved performance, especially in the dark, suggesting that it had an alerting effect. There were also more false alarms with this condition. The horn acted as a negative reinforcement for too cautious a criterion, and also gave the subjects information about their performance.

A number of workers have examined the effect of giving K R on a proportion of the signals. This has the advantage that extra signals can be injected into a real task, and feedback given on these extra or artificial signals. It has been found that such partial K R improves performance on the 'real' signals which are not followed by K R. Garvey et al. (1959) indicated when 'artificial' signals had been missed by a light or a loud noise. There was an over-all improvement in performance with the light, and the loud noise increased performance even more. This again suggests an arousal effect for the noise, since it did not add any further information. A similar experiment was carried out by Baker (1960b). Subjects were informed by headphones when they missed the dot of light that was an 'artificial' signal. There were sixteen 'artificial' signals and twenty-four 'real' signals which were the same as the artificial ones. Subjects were also told when they gave a false alarm. K R improved performance throughout.

The proportion of signals on which K R was given was varied from 0 to 100 per cent by Johnson and Payne (1966). The signal was a vertical deflection of a horizontal trace that moved ten times a minute across the face of an oscilloscope. Feedback was given by telling the subject when a signal had occurred. It was found that the over-all level of detection was markedly increased by adding 25 per cent K R and even more by higher proportions. K R had no effect, however, on the decrement in detection, which was the same for all conditions.

Motivation

The motivating effect of feedback was studied by Baker (1961), who told the subjects that they would receive information on their performance on a secondary task, responding to a change in the ambient lighting or noise. These instructions improved performance on the main detection task from the very beginning, before any signals had been given on the secondary task. It is clear that in this case the knowledge that they would receive this secondary information had a purely motivating effect.

False K R may have both a motivating and a dishabituating effect but presumably cannot give any information about the actual distribution, though it does tell the subject that there are more signals than he has responded to. Thus, a study of the difference between true K R and false K R can help to disentangle these different aspects. A comparison of true and false K R was made by Weidenfeller *et al.* (1962). The subjects were told by a light when they had missed a 0·03 second inter-ruption of a continuous light. With false K R, this feedback light flashed when no signal had occurred. There were no significant differences between the two K R conditions, which showed very little decrement in detection over the three hours of the test. There were two control conditions, both of which showed considerable decrement in detections during the session. In one of these conditions, the K R light flashed but the subjects were told that it was irrelevant. There was no difference in detections between this and the control condition without a light. The experiment demonstrated that the motivating and alerting effect of an apparently meaningful stimulus was as effective as true K R. When the extra stimulus was not meaningful, it had no effect.

A further study on the effects of false K R was carried out by J. F. Mackworth (1964). K R was given by a red light that came on two seconds after a signal had been given and not reported. With false K R, the light came on twice in each ten-minute period, at random time intervals. This was the same as the average number of times that the true K R light appeared. Both true and false K R produced an over-all im-provement in detections and in d' (see Figure 16). There was very little decrement during the session with K R, but with false K R the rate of decrement was about the same as that found with the control. False alarms were increased with both types of KR, suggesting that a more lax criterion was produced by information about missed signals. In control sessions following the KR sessions, there was evidence of

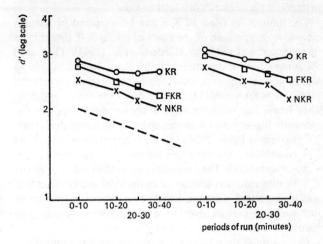

KR Knowledge of results
FKR False knowledge of results
NKR No knowledge of results
— — d' slope (exp. 1 J. F. Mackworth and Taylor, 1963)

Figure 16 The effect of knowledge and false knowledge of results on the detectability of a signal. The left-hand data are compiled from group percentages, while the right-hand data are compiled from values for d' calculated for individual Ss. Data from the Continuous Clock test (J. F. Mackworth, 1964)

definite improvement, while no significant improvement was found between sessions when no KR was given in any of them. A somewhat doubtful improvement was found in control sessions following false KR, but this improvement between first and last control sessions with intervening false KR sessions was less than that found with intervening true KR sessions. It was concluded that false KR would share with true K R the alerting, motivating or dishabituating effect; in addition, true K R might permit some learning which would act both to reduce the rate of decrement during the session and to improve performance in a later session.

The motivating effect of K R can be increased by various means. A comparison of the effect of giving K R by lights or by intercom was made by Hardesty *et al.* (1963). They used the Jump Clock and presented full K R on detections, missed signals and false alarms, thus copying the original experiment by N. H. Mackworth (1950) and adding the extra condition. They found that the percentage of correct detections was significantly higher when K R was given by intercom than when it was given by lights. While there was less decrement with the K R conditions, this difference between K R and the control was not significant. The motivating or alerting effect of giving K R by intercom was additional to the informative effect that was also present with the lights. This improvement due to the intercom carried over to a later control session (see Figures 17a and 17b).

Other studies on motivation have separated the immediate effect of K R within a session from reward for good performance given after the session. Sipowicz *et al.* (1962) studied the effect of K R for missed signals and later reward in a task requiring detection of a brief pause in a continuous light. In the reward condition, the subjects were told that they would be given three dollars if they detected all the signals and would lose five cents if they missed one, with a doubled loss for each further signal that they missed. Subjects missed 24 per cent of signals in the control condition, 12 per cent with K R alone, 8 per cent with reward alone and 4 per cent with both K R and reward. Significant decrement in detection during the session was found only with the control condition. There were no significant differences in false alarms, but few were given with the K R and reward condition, while most were given with the K R condition. It would therefore appear that sensitivity was improved by the reward. While subjects may have made more observing responses with the reward

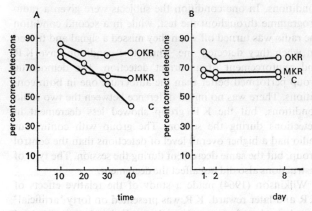

Figure 17a Per cent signals correctly detected during
successive ten-minute periods in the initial test day. Each curve
represents a different mode of presenting knowledge of
results: C represents the control condition (no knowledge of
results); O K R represents the observer-presented verbal report;
and M K R represents the presentation of knowledge of results
by means of signal lights in the visual display
Figure 17b Per cent signals correctly detected on three
successive test days. On the initial day performance was
under different modes of presenting knowledge of results
(C, O K R, M K R). On days 2 and 8 all groups were tested
without knowledge of results (Hardesty, Trumbo and Bevan,
1963)

condition, there must also have been a change in their efficiency
in detecting the signals; otherwise there would have been an
increase in false alarms. It would seem that the activating
effect of reward was more powerful than the effect of any
information about the task given by the K R.

A further study on motivation in the same task was carried
out by Ware, Kowal and Baker (1964). Their subjects were
divided into two groups, one of which was treated by the
experimenter in an autocratic manner, while the other was
treated in a democratic way, receiving more information and
being allowed to decide the order in which they received the

conditions. In one condition the subjects were given a radio programme throughout the test, while in a second condition the radio was turned off when they missed a signal and turned on when they detected one. Thus, this condition gave K R and reinforcement of a correct detection. The democratic group performed better than the autocratic one in both conditions. There was no initial difference between the two radio conditions, but the K R group showed less decrement in detections during the session. The group with continuous radio had a higher overall level of detections than the control group, but the same decrement during the session. The type of instructions also did not affect the decrement.

Wilkinson (1964) made a study of the relative effects of K R and later reward. K R was presented on forty 'artificial' signals, and performance on eight 'real' signals was examined with and without the extra forty signals. The signals were shorter pulses in a series of auditory pulses occurring at twenty per minute. K R consisted of hit or miss information (part K R). The extra reward was given by posting the results on the notice-board after the session (full K R). The results showed that there was an improvement in detections of both the real and the artificial signals when K R was added to the latter. Table 1 (see p. 43) presents some calculations made from the reported data. The percentage of detections from the total number of signals presented under the various conditions is shown, as well as the data for the eight real signals in the control condition in which only these signals were given. It is interesting that while there appears to be a fall in d' and a decrease in *beta* during the session with the eight signals alone, the more usual finding of no change in d' and a marked increase in *beta* appears with the forty-eight signal condition.

There was an increase in false alarms during the session with K R, suggesting that when subjects are not directly informed about false alarms, they tend to relax their criterion. (A similar increase in false alarms with K R was reported by J. F. Mackworth, 1964.) The data also suggest an increase in d' with K R as compared with the control. The addition of final publication of the results gives an even greater change in all measures, increased detections, false alarms, and values for d', with decreased values for *beta*. These data can be explained on the assumption that subjects made more 'observing responses'. They can also be explained on the assumption that because subjects paid more attention to the tones, therefore the potentials evoked by these tones were larger, thus leading to more detections and more false alarms (see J. F. Mackworth, 1969). At the same time increased arousal led to increased ability to discriminate the signal. In other words, the extra motivation led to changes that were the reverse of those found in the control vigilance task.

In alternating sessions all groups were tested with the eight real signals alone and no K R. Those groups that received K R on the artificial signals showed better detection in the intervening control sessions than those who did not. Thus it would seem that they had learned something about the signal. It is, however, possible that there would be a carry-over of arousal and interest in the task from the K R sessions. The decrement in detection during these intervening control sessions was the same with the K R and no-K R groups.

Learning was also seen with the K R groups, who improved from the second to the sixth session, while the group who had no K R showed no such improvement. The group who received full K R performed at a very high level throughout. This again emphasizes the importance of motivation.

Another study of the non-informative aspects of K R was carried out by Ware and Baker (1964). They found that there were more detections of a pause in a continuous light when K R was given verbally than when it was given non-verbally; auditory K R was better than visual; and with the non-verbal K R, results were better when subjects were told that they had missed a signal than when they were told only that their response was correct.

In a study by Bergum and Lehr (1964), motivation was studied without immediate K R. One group of subjects was told that they would receive twenty cents for each correct detection and lose twenty cents for each omission. This group detected more signals than the control group at the beginning of the session, but after twenty minutes there was no difference between the groups. In a later session, no reward was offered and the group that had received the reward previously now showed a much greater decrement than the control group. The task required the detection of a missing light in a circle of lights lit in sequence at 12 r.p.m. In a previous experiment, Bergum and Lehr (1963c) had found that KR made no significant difference in the decrement in detections. It is possible that the very high event rate (240 per minute) leads to 'blurring' and decreased detectability (see chapter 3).

The Nature of the Feedback

Feedback can be given in three ways. The subject can be informed whether or not his response is correct. From this he knows how many correct and incorrect responses he makes, but not how many signals he has missed. He can be informed when he has missed a signal, but will not know when he has made a false positive. Finally, he can be given both these kinds of KR. It may also make a difference if he is told when he has made a false response, even though this conveys the same information as being told his correct responses, because an emphasis on false alarms may lead to a more strict criterion, or on the other hand, the subject may deliberately relax his criterion in order to get some information about his performance.

Wiener (1963) examined the detection of signals on the Jump Clock, with three levels of KR and three signal rates (sixteen, thirty-two and forty-eight per hour). The three levels of KR were no KR, KRC (correct detections and false alarms) or full KR (KRC plus missed signals). Maximal detection and minimal false alarms were found with full KR, and there was no decrement during the session with this condition. It would seem that full KR increased the ability of the observer to detect the signal, as reported above with the data from Wilkinson (1964) and J. F. Mackworth (1964). With K R C, more signals were detected than with the control, but there were also many more false alarms (except with the slowest signal rate). It would therefore seem that the effect of feedback only on positive responses resulted in a less cautious criterion (or perhaps increased the evoked potentials produced by the repetitive jumps). When K R is given on missed signals, then as the observer gives fewer responses and misses more signals, the feedback increases, while with the K R C condition, feedback decreases as positive responses decrease. Therefore, the alerting effect is maximal with full K R, which may result in increased discrimination due to decrease in the neural noise.

In the second session of this experiment, all groups received thirty-two signals per hour and no K R. Both K R groups detected more signals than the group who had received no K R in the first session. The false alarms followed the same pattern as in the first session. Thus, it appeared that both the change in sensitivity and the change in criterion carried over to the second session without K R (see also Wiener, 1967, 1968; Wiener and Attwood, 1968).

The three kinds of K R, hits, missed signals and false alarms, were studied by Chinn and Alluisi (1964) in a $2 \times 2 \times 2$ factorial design. The task required detection of an out-of-sequence flash in a series of two lights flashing alternately. The dependent variable was the over-all level of performance. It was found that hit K R increased detections and produced a small decrease in false alarms, suggesting that there was an improvement in sensitivity. False-alarm K R significantly decreased the number of false alarms and also increased the number of missed signals, suggesting that the effect of feedback on false alarms alone was to produce a more cautious criterion. Missed signal K R also significantly decreased false alarms. Since there was no significant effect of missed signal K R on detections, it is possible that here, also, there was some improvement in sensitivity, but the result is somewhat unexpected. The authors suggested that negative reinforcement following a response tends to lower the probability of that event. They pointed out that information about hits *or* false alarms would tell the subject whether or not his responses were correct, but these conditions differ in the nature of the reinforcement. Negative reinforcement of false alarms leads to a more cautious performance, while positive reinforcement of hits leads to an increased sensitivity.

A comparison of the effects of two kinds of K R was also made by Bevan and Turner (1965) using an auditory task in which there was no decrement during the session even in the control. K R (reinforcement) consisted in *either* giving a penny immediately after each correct detection *or* a shock after each missed signal. The two kinds of reinforcement were equally effective in improving detections. In another condition the reinforcement was changed in the middle of the session. Subjects knew that this change would occur. These subjects detected more signals right from the beginning of the session than the other group receiving the same reinforcement but not anticipating change. This result was reminiscent of the finding by C. H. Baker (1961) that detection was better even before any K R about a secondary task had been received.

Learning

Several of the studies described above have indicated that improvements in detection probability can be found in later sessions as a result of K R in a previous session (N. H. Mackworth, 1950; Wiener, 1963; J. F. Mackworth, 1964; Wilkinson, 1964). The use of K R for training was also studied by O'Hanlon *et al.* (1965). They used a sonar task and flashed a green light or 'indicator' when a correct detection was made. When a subject had missed two or three signals, he was given an 'artificial signal' and a green or red light indicated whether he detected or missed this 'artificial' signal. The indicator increased both detections and false alarms. Thus it appeared that its main effect was to encourage a more relaxed criterion. It was, however, found that performance in the post-test was significantly better following the indicator than following the control condition. It was found that those subjects who were poorest in the control condition showed most improvement with the indicator. A cross-over design was employed, but data were not given for the two watches separately.

Other workers have failed to find any lasting effect of K R upon performance (e.g. Bergum and Lehr, 1963c). Loeb and Binford (1964) presented K R as a click following every signal in an auditory task. Half the subjects received K R in the initial training session and half did not. Three sessions without K R followed. In all sessions the subjects who had received K R initially detected fewer signals and gave fewer false alarms than those who were trained without K R. The decreases in detections and in false alarms during each session were about the same in both groups. Both groups showed an improvement in detections and a decrease in false alarms between early and late sessions. It appeared that the main function of K R in this experiment was to produce a more cautious criterion.

Absence of effect of K R both during a session and in a later session without K R was also found by Colquhoun (1966a), using a task that required detection of a larger disc among a set of six. Neither the groups with K R nor with cueing showed any advantage over the control condition in either session. In all groups there was little change in detections over sessions, but a decrease in false responses. Thus the sensitivity (d') improved and the criterion became more cautious with repeated sessions. All subjects were given a 'pre-training' session, with full knowledge of results and the same signal distribution as the main sessions. Colquhoun suggested that this pre-training gave the subjects adequate knowledge of the signal characteristics, and that the further improvement in detectability perhaps resulted from learning to use more systematic patterns of search.

Reaction time

In reaction time experiments, the subject normally detects almost all the signals. Therefore, feedback usually consists of a comparison of the speed of response with previous responses by the same subject. This feedback gives no knowledge of the task, but does emphasize any changes in the alertness of the subject. Thus the motivating aspect of KR is here almost the only effect. The results have been quite consistent in showing improvement due to KR.

Subjects responding to a brief light were given a green light to indicate a faster response than the previous one, and a red light to indicate a slower response (McCormack, 1959; McCormack *et al.*, 1962). The increase in RT during the control session was either reduced or absent in the KR condition. In a third condition, both KR lights were lit after every response. This condition was not significantly different from the control. Thus the KR lights were only effective when they had a meaning for the subject. The relation between intersignal interval and KR was also examined. The control condition showed maximum RT following the shortest interval and minimum RT following the second longest interval (75 seconds). With KR the shortest RT followed the mean interval (60 seconds). The maximal effect of KR was on the responses following the shorter intervals. This might be explained in terms of arousal. Expectancy tends to decrease latency as the intersignal interval increases, but arousal resulting from KR following a signal would naturally tend to be at its highest immediately after the signal.

McCormack and colleagues also found that if KR was given on 30 per cent or more of the signals, there was no increase in RT during the session (McCormack, Binding and McElheran, 1963). When KR was given on 20 per cent or fewer of the signals, there was some increase in RT during the session (McCormack and McElheran, 1963).

Similar results were found when KR was given in an auditory task. Loeb and Schmidt (1963) presented tones at 60dB and 10dB above threshold. With 60dB there were no significant changes in RT during the session. With 10dB there was an increase, which could be prevented by giving information by lights about the speed of response. False KR was given to a group which was told that the lights indicated their relative speed of response but, in fact, the lights appeared randomly. This group showed a slight increase in R T. The greatest increase in R T was found with a group that received an 'acknowledge' light after each response. There was a slight increase in missed signals during the sessions; this decrement in detection was the same in all conditions.

Both these experiments show that the lights have to be meaningful to maintain performance. Repetitive stimuli have very little effect on arousal unless they carry information.

The use of K R as a training method was demonstrated by Adams and Humes (1963). They presented a complex display with six symbols moving at different speeds. The signal was a change of one symbol from G to F. One group was given K R in the first session, followed by two sessions without K R. Another group received three sessions without K R. The first group showed faster responses in all sessions than the second. There was an increase in R T during all sessions.

It was found by Hardesty and Bevan (1964) that quantitative information about the exact time of response was more effective than simple comments as to the direction of performance, but the best performance was found when both types of K R were given together.

The effect of K R, and differential monetary rewards, on speed of response was examined by Montague and Webber (1965). K R was given by four lights, indicating three levels of performance: superior, defined as faster than 750 milliseconds; adequate, 760–1750 milliseconds; and poor. Increases in R T during the criterion session were found with all conditions. The fastest mean R Ts were found with the condition in which both K R and reward were given in both training and criterion sessions. No other significant differences were found, although the control condition showed a lower average speed of response than the others. Perhaps the absence of K R effect was due to the fact that the subject's performance was not compared directly with his own previous responses, so that it was difficult for him to assess his own change in alertness. Performance in the criterion session without KR and reward was not improved when these conditions were given in the training session.

Other tasks

The effect of various kinds of KR on performance in a tracking task was examined by Hauty and Payne (1955). The subjects worked for successive one-minute trials, separated by fifteen-second pauses, at a task requiring four pointers to be kept in null position. The operator could see for himself the results of his activity, but extra KR was given in two conditions. Either a light or a tone indicated that all the pointers were on target. The decrement in performance was the same in all conditions, but the over-all level was maximal with the tone, and intermediate with the visual KR. This difference between tone and light would suggest an arousing effect, since a tone would be more arousing than a light in a well-lit task.

The effects of KR, sleep-loss and noise on performance in the self-paced five-choice serial reaction test were reported by Wilkinson (1961a, 1963). In the KR condition, KR was given as a bell following an error, a buzz given when there was a 1·5 second gap between one response and the next, and the publication of scores. Subjects were tested for six weeks, twice a week. All subjects received the four combinations of sleep and KR every two weeks. There were interactions between the three variables of sleep, KR and sessions. KR had a greater effect on the performance of the sleepless subjects than when they were rested. Decreases in the rate of correct responses and increases in positive errors were found in all sessions. KR reduced both these changes. When the test followed a night without sleep, the most noticeable effect was a rise in the number of 1·5-second gaps as time on task increased. During the first four weeks, KR almost completely prevented this increase in gaps, but in the last two weeks there was some increase in gaps even when KR was given.

Noise slightly improved performance by the sleepless

subjects. The beneficial effect of K R on gaps was greater when the test was carried out in quiet. The addition of noise to K R increased the positive errors. Wilkinson (1963) concluded that both noise and K R were arousing, while loss of sleep led to low arousal in a prolonged and monotonous task. K R and noise together might lead to hyper-arousal.

Wilkinson (1962) also examined the effect of K R and sleep-loss on the speed of mental arithmetic. All subjects worked on the arithmetic for fifteen minutes and then received K R in the form of comments by the experimenter on their speed and accuracy. Normal subjects improved their speed during the first fifteen minutes, while the sleep-deprived subjects showed a considerable reduction in speed. When K R was given, the sleep-deprived subjects improved their speed, while the control subjects actually became slower, so that there was no difference between the two groups.

Measurements of the electromyographic level (E M G) were taken during the tests. Both groups showed an increase in E M G when K R was given; the increase was greater with the control group, suggesting that this group, already working at their most efficient arousal level, were hyper-aroused by the feedback. This illustrates the U-shaped relation between arousal and performance. Wilkinson pointed out, however, that the relation of E M G and performance was not simple, because some of the sleepless subjects showed very high levels of E M G and also showed good performance. Wilkinson suggested that these subjects put out extra effort in order to maintain performance when suffering from loss of sleep.

A relationship has been demonstrated between R T, the evoked potential and the effect of K R upon these two measures. Donchin and Lindsley (1966) found an increase in R T during a task requiring response to a flash. This increase in R T was accompanied by an increase in the latency of the negative component of the evoked potential and a decrease in the amplitude. When verbal K R was given by the experimenter R T decreased, and the amplitude of the potential increased.

Summary and Conclusions

In the majority of the experiments, knowledge of results improved performance, especially towards the end of the session. Feedback was given in two main forms during the tasks. In one the subject was informed of the accuracy of his response; in the other, he was told about the speed of response. Information about the accuracy of discrimination can give the subject knowledge about the signal, its physical nature and temporal probability. Information about speed of response tells the subject whether he is improving or deteriorating, and helps to maintain his alertness. Both kinds of information can have a motivating effect, and it is probable that this is the most important aspect of feedback in these tasks, where there is no requirement for muscular skill.

The influence of feedback is to be expected from all theories of vigilance behaviour. A strong extra stimulus will produce *dishabituation* of the arousal response and the evoked potential, but this effect will habituate rapidly unless the extra stimulus is meaningful for the subject. The motivating effect of K R will also help to maintain the general level of arousal. The effects of amphetamine, K R and false K R have been compared (J. F. Mackworth, 1965a). K R and false K R both increase the overall level of performance, from the beginning of the session, while amphetamine and K R both reduce the decrement in detections. The effects of K R and amphetamine may be additive. False alarms are increased with K R and false K R, but are unaffected or reduced with amphetamine (see J. F. Mackworth, 1969). Habituation of the arousal response may result in *increased* neural noise, hence there may be decreased detectability with increased or unchanged false alarms. Amphetamine would act mainly to prevent this change. Habituation of the evoked potential may result in a decrease in detections and false alarms, leading to an apparent change in criterion. K R may act to prevent this change. Reinforcement of the signal or response to it may increase the dishabituating effect of the signal.

The *expectancy theory* explains the effect of K R as giving the subject information about the temporal distribution of the signals. This may result in an absence of effect of K R when the subject is already fully aware of the distribution. Such an explanation is not applicable to reaction-time tasks. There is evidence that the improvement produced by K R will carry over to a later session without K R. This would appear to be due to learning the characteristics of the signal, including the temporal probability. Changes in detectability and in criterion established by K R are also found in a later session.

The effect of *motivation* has been shown in a number of experiments. The way in which the K R is given is influential, verbal comments being more effective than non-verbal feedback. Rewards following the session also have a marked effect on performance in certain cases. This effect appears to be not only on the criterion but also on the detectability of the signal. Similarly, false knowledge of results improves detectability, but does not prevent the decrement in detection during the session.

Criterial changes are also affected by K R. The usual decrease in false alarms, and increase in caution, may be counteracted, especially if feedback is given only about correct detections or missed signals. On the other hand, when feedback is given only on false alarms, the usual increases in caution may be exaggerated.

The description of vigilance changes in terms of the *observing response* also accords well with the data. K R will act by increasing the neural response to the repetitive events so that the cost of an observing response is lower, and by increasing the cost of a failure to observe a signal and the reward of observing one. The finding that there is a different effect when feedback is not contingent on performance, but is simply a statement that a signal has occurred, emphasizes the importance of the reinforcement of performance.

In conclusion, knowledge of results produces an improvement in vigilance tasks. This may be seen either as a decrease in missed signals or in the latency of response. There may be

Table 4
A Summary of Some Experiments on Knowledge of Results in Vigilance Tasks

Authors	Mode*	Variables	KR on		Results			
			Hit	Miss F.A.**	1	2	3	4***
N. H. Mackworth, 1950	V	Verbal KR	+	+ +		+	+	
	A	Verbal KR	+	+ +		+	+	
Pollack and Knaff, 1958	V	Horn KR, reward lighting		+	+			+ (horn)
Garvey, Taylor and Newling, 1959	V	Artificial signals	+ or	+	+ +	0		
C. H. Baker, 1960	V	40 per cent KR	+	+	+ +	=		
C. H. Baker, 1961	V	Second task		+	+ +	0		
Weidenfeller, Baker and Ware, 1962	V	KR, false KR	+	+		+		
Sipowicz, Ware and Baker, 1962	V	KR, reward	+	+ +	+	+ +		=
Hardesty, Trumbo and Bevan, 1963	V	KR, lights intercom	+	+ +	+	+ +		(±)
Bergum and Lehr, 1963	V	50–100 per cent KR	+	+ +	+	=	+	
Bergum and Lehr, 1964	V	Reward	+	±		=	−	
Wiener, 1963	V	Part/full KR	+	+ +	+ +	+ +	+ +	
J. F. Mackworth, 1964	V	KR, false KR		+ +	+ +	+ +		
Ware, Kowal and Baker, 1964	V	KR radio, instructions	+	+		+		+
Wilkinson, 1964	A	KR 80 per cent,						

Reference	*	K R	1	2	3	4	** F.A.
[...]r and Baker, 1964	V	K R, A, v, verbal	+				+
Chinn and Alluisi, 1964	V	varied K R	±	±	–	=	+
Loeb and Binford, 1964	A	click after signal	+	±	+	=	–
O'Hanlon, Schmidt and Baker, 1965	A	K R on extra signal	+	+	+	+	+
Bevan and Turner, 1965	A	Penny/shock	+	–	±		0
Johnson and Payne, 1966	V	0–100 per cent	+	+	=		0
Colquhoun, 1966	V	K R, cueing	+	+–	+=	+	=

Response speed

Reaction time experiments

Reference	*	K R	Response speed
McCormack, 1959	V	Visual K R on speed	+
McCormack, Binding and McElheran, 1963	V	0–100 per cent K R	+ (K R 30 per cent up)
Loeb and Schmidt, 1963	A	K R, false K R	+
Adams and Humes, 1963	V	Sessions	=
Hardesty and Bevan, 1964	V	K R comments or time	+
Montague and Webber, 1965	V	K R lights, payment	+

Key

* V = Visual; A = Auditory modes.

** F.A. = False alarms.

*** 1 = Effect of K R on over-all level of detections. +, increased level.

2 = Effect of K R on decrement in detections during session. +, reduced or absent decrement. =, no effect on decrement. 0, no decrement in control.

3 = Effect on detections in later sessions without K R. +, improved detection. =, no effect. —, fewer detections.

4 = Change in false alarms. +, increased number. =, no effect. = reduced number.

an over-all improvement with some decrement during the session, but usually there is no decrement during a session with K R. These changes may be due to (1) learning the characteristics of the signal, (2) a prevention of the usual increase in caution, (3) reinforcement, or increasing the rewards of observing and the penalties of non-observing, (4) the alerting or dishabituating effect of strong extra-meaningful stimuli, and (5) other motivational effects which encourage the subject to try to keep himself awake. A summary of the data appears in Table 4 on pages 128-9

7 Recovery between Testing

Speculations on the causes of the vigilance decrement must take into account the effect of intervening periods during which the subject is not being required to carry out his task. Such rest pauses may vary from a few seconds to several days. In almost every case even a brief rest is sufficient to produce a considerable improvement in performance. A short break in a series of repeated stimuli may result in complete dishabituation, but it is not easy to see why such a break might lead to changes in expectancy or criterion.

There is, however, one major difference between habituation of the response to a stimulus that does not require a response, and the effect of multiple sessions on a vigilance task. In the first case, the rate and over-all level of habituation will increase from day to day, until eventually there is no physiological response to the unimportant stimuli. But in a vigilance task, it has usually been found that there is either no reduction or an improvement in performance from day to day. Thus, it must be considered that in addition to habituation of the neural response to the non-signal events, there is also some learning about the nature and probability of the signal. For instance, while there may be a marked improvement in detections between the end of one session and the beginning of the next, false alarms may fail to show an equivalent rise to the initial level.

Multiple Sessions

Incomplete recovery

Several experiments have shown less than complete recovery between sessions. N. H. Mackworth (1950) found that the initial level of detection was lower in the second session than in the first, in the three kinds of tests that he studied – the Jump Clock Test, the Radar Test and the Listening Test. The rate of decrement was the same in the two successive sessions in both the Clock Test and the Radar Test, so that the overall level of performance was poorer in the second session in both these tests. In the Listening Test, however, the decrement was less in the second session, so that there was no difference between the overall levels for the two sessions. Jenkins (1958) also found that detections at the beginning of the second, afternoon, session on a meter deflection task were fewer than at the beginning of the first, morning, session, and the over-all level of performance was poorer in the second session.

Decreases in the initial level of detections were also found by C. H. Baker (1963b), in the second session on the Continuous Clock, and by Buckner et al. (1960, 1965), in successive weeks on a visual vigilance task (see Figure 18). In both tasks the overall level improved from day to day over five sessions. Buckner et al. (1960) found, however, a considerable decrease in detections in the session following three days' rest. It would appear that too long a period between tests resulted in forgetting what had been learned about the signal. On the other hand, Buckner et al. (1960, 1965) found in an auditory task that there was a decrease in performance from day to day but an improvement between the first and second weeks of testing. They found that false alarms were maximal on the first day, and decreased rapidly over the first three days, reaching a very low and stable level.

Complete recovery

A number of workers have found that there was complete recovery between sessions and no significant differences between sessions. Adams and his colleagues examined performance in a latency task. Adams, Humes and Stenson (1962) found no significant differences between sessions on nine

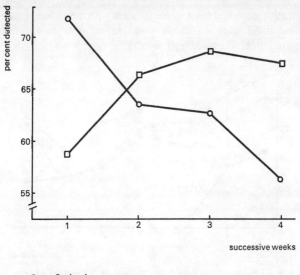

O——O visual
□——□ auditory

Figure18 Mean percentage detections by mode as a function of weeks on watch (Buckner, Harabedian and McGrath, 1965)

successive days, with a further test seven days later. Further tests, however, with this same scanning task showed improvements between sessions (Adams and Humes, 1963; Adams, Humes and Sieveking, 1963).

Wiener (1964a) examined the effect of training subjects with signals of different levels of difficulty. On the second day, all the subjects were tested with the medium level (see Figure 19). Those subjects who had received the medium signal on both days showed complete recovery between sessions. This group performed better than the other two groups who had received signals that were easier or more difficult than those with which they had been trained. There was, however, no significant difference between the groups. In the training period most false alarms were given by the subjects with the most difficult signal, and least by the subjects with the easiest signal. These differences in false alarms carried over to the test session, though considerably reduced.

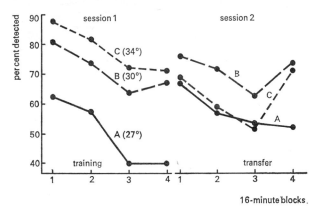

Figure 19 Percentage of detected signals as a function of time and signal amplitude in session 1 and session 2. In session 2, all groups ran under signal amplitude B, but are designated by their session 1 (training) signal amplitude (Wiener, 1964a)

The effect of repeated sessions on the Mackworth Jump Clock was examined by Hardesty et al. (1963), using a range of signal intervals from 30 to 180 seconds. On the first day, one group received knowledge of results by lights, and another group received oral knowledge of results. There was no significant difference between the control group and the group receiving visual knowledge of results, though the data suggested a larger decrement over time with the control condition. The group with oral knowledge of results detected more signals on this first test and also on two subsequent tests without knowledge of results. There was no significant difference between sessions. The authors pointed out that the motivational effect of verbal knowledge of results could produce a lasting improvement (see Figures 17a and 17b, p. 115).

Absence of significant differences between days with visual tasks was also found by J. F. Mackworth (1964), and R. A. Baker *et al.* (1961). The same result was found in auditory tasks by Ware, Sipowicz and Baker (1961), and Webb and Wherry (1960). Wilkinson (1964) also found no improvement between sessions in an auditory task when there was no feedback in any session.

Broadbent and Gregory (1965) found in a visual task that there was no significant change in the detectability of the signal (d') between successive days, but there was a change in the trend of the criterion, as measured by *beta*. On the first day there was an increase in *beta* during the session, but on the second day there was no significant change. Thus it would appear that on the first day subjects became definitely more cautious during the session. This might suggest that subjects were still learning about the signal distribution in the first test, even though they had already received a training session with the same signal distribution.

Improved performance

Colquhoun examined the effect of training in several experiments. As mentioned previously, Adams and Humes (1963) and Adams, Humes and Sieveking (1963) found an increased speed of response in consecutive sessions on a complex visual task that involved scanning. Colquhoun (1966a) suggested a similar explanation for improvement between sessions in a task requiring search for a possible larger disc in each set of six discs. No improvements in detection probabilities were found between sessions, but there was a decrease in false alarms. Thus there was an apparent increase in detectability and in caution, as indicated by *beta*, between sessions. Colquhoun suggested that the increase in caution might be due either to a continuing adjustment of the subject's subjective probability of signal occurrence towards the actual probability, or to a progressive change in the 'detection' goal of the subject, determined by the values or costs which he associates with his decision. As in the experiment by Broadbent and Gregory (1965), all subjects received an initial session with full knowledge of results and the same signal probability as in the test sessions.

Colquhoun and Baddeley (1964) examined the effect of expectancy due to pretraining by varying the signal rate in each of two successive sessions in a visual vigilance task. Colquhoun and Baddeley (1967) repeated the experimental design with an auditory vigilance task. They found that subjects who were trained with the high signal rate detected more signals in the test session with either high or low signal rates. Those who were trained with the high rate and tested with the low rate showed the greatest decrement in detections during the test session. This group also gave most false alarms, but showed a decline during the session, resulting in a highly significant rise in *beta*. There were no significant differences between the groups in d', the detectability of the signal, but *beta*, the index of caution, was higher with the group trained with the low signal rate. It was therefore clear that the training signal rate affected the caution of the observer, not his sensitivity to the signal. Colquhoun and Baddeley regarded these results as supporting the expectancy theory. It would, however, appear that one practice session is insufficient to establish the criterion at a stable level.

Improvements in detection in successive sessions in an auditory task have been found by several workers. Alluisi and Hall (1963) found an improvement between the first and second session, but the performance level in the fourth session was the same as in the first. Buckner *et al.* (1960, 1965) found an improvement between the first and second weeks of testing (see Figure 18 above). Elliott (1957) tested the effective threshold for auditory tones in noise and found a continuous improvement over sessions.

A careful examination of the effect of repeated sessions on detections in an auditory vigilance task was made by Binford

Table 5

Changes in d' and *beta* within and between Sessions in an Auditory Vigilance Task (adapted from Binford and Loeb, 1966)

Number of criteria	Session	d' 20 min period		beta 20 min period	
		First	Last	First	Last
Multiple	1 and 2	3·09	2·96	13·72	26·88
	8 and 9	3·58	3·43	43·41	42·28
Single	1 and 2	2·54	2·48	17·74	129·68
	8 and 9	3·93	3·18	54·80	87·92

and Loeb (1966). They found a considerable improvement in detections in later sessions, but no change in the decrement during the session. False alarms began at a high level in the first session but fell off rapidly. In later sessions, false alarms were very few, but increased slightly during the session. In the early sessions, the changes in d' were not significant, but *beta* showed a significant increase. In the later sessions, d' was initially much higher but showed a significant decrement during the session. The criterial level, as indicated by *beta*, was higher at the beginning of the later sessions than at the beginning of the early sessions but showed no significant changes during the later sessions (see Table 5). This experiment suggests that there are two kinds of changes taking place in a vigilance task. It would appear that changes in *criterion* occur mainly in the early sessions, while subjects are adjusting their criterion to suit the signal probability that they find. Once learning, about the distribution of the signals and also about the differentiation of the signal from the noise, has reached a maximum, there remains a decrement in both detections and in d' during the session (see Figure 20).

McGrath (1960) reported that in a visual vigilance task there was an improvement from day to day. The percentage of detections increased and the percentage of false alarms decreased considerably between the first and subsequent days. Thus it would appear that there was an increase in the sensitivity of the subjects for the signals, as measured by d'.

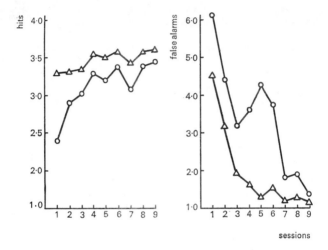

o single criterion

Δ multiple criteria

Figure 20 Number of hits and false alarms in an auditory vigilance task in successive sessions. Single criterion represents the usual vigilance condition of pressing a button whenever a signal was detected. With the multiple criterion, subjects had to select one of three buttons to indicate their degree of confidence (Binford and Loeb, 1966)

These data suggest that during the first few sessions the subject is learning the probabilities of the signal, and adjusting his criterion accordingly; he is also learning to distinguish the signal from the background events, so that an improvement in sensitivity or latency may become apparent between sessions.

These two processes may counteract each other to some extent.

It is possible that the neural evoked response to the background events of the task shows less recovery between sessions than the arousal or orienting response. Moreover, the general level of arousal will be quite high at the beginning of successive sessions. It has been pointed out that the sensitivity of the subject for a small difference between background events and the signal event may be improved by an increase in arousal, but may also be improved by a *decrease* in the evoked potential response to the background events. On the other hand, a decrease in the evoked response may result in a decrease in both correct detections and in false alarms. Only a study of the relation between these two neurological measures and performance in successive sessions can disentangle the complex possibilities.

Rest Pauses

In view of the finding that performance shows a marked improvement between the end of one session and the beginning of the next, it is of interest to inquire how brief this intervening period can be for complete recovery.

N. H. Mackworth (1950) tested subjects with half-hour spells of work alternating with half-hours of rest. He found that there was no significant difference between the periods of work. Rest for half-an-hour completely restored performance. Jenkins (1958) turned off the display and sounded a tone every five minutes. The rest pauses lasted for thirty seconds. Performance remained high during the ninety minutes of the test. It made no difference whether subjects remained in their seats or left the rooms and exercised. Such findings support the concept that the decrement is due to habituation rather than to changes in expectancy.

The effect of rest may depend on both the length of the test period and the duration of the rest pause. McCormack (1958) tested subjects in a reaction-time task for forty minutes, and then gave them a rest of five or ten minutes, followed by a further ten minutes of testing. There was a steady increase in reaction time during continuous testing, with some recovery over five minutes' rest, and nearly twice as much over ten minutes. Colquhoun (1959) examined the effect of a pause of five minutes after thirty minutes of testing on an inspection task in which thirty-four out of fifty 'strips' given in each minute were faulty. The subjects who were tested continuously for an hour showed a decrease in detections during the second half-hour, but those subjects who had five minutes' rest at the end of the first half-hour maintained their level of performance throughout. Ten-minute rest pauses were given by Bergum and Lehr (1962a) after each half-hour of a visual vigilance task. Performance remained stable over ninety minutes of testing when rest pauses were given, but deteriorated in the second half-hour when they were not.

The effect of different kinds of activity during five-minute rest pauses was examined by Bevan *et al.* (1967). There was a decrement in detections in a visual vigilance task during the ninety minutes of the continuous task. No decrement was found when rest pauses were given every half-hour and filled with either exercises, anagrams or sensory restriction. Thus the important aspect of the rest pause would appear to be the absence of the vigilance task, suggesting that habituation of the neural response to the repetitive stimulus is the cause of the decrement.

These results suggest that an alternation of monitors would be a useful way to maintain performance. A study of such an alternation was carried out by Ware, Baker and Drucker (1964), who reached the surprising conclusion that performance was not improved by alternating monitors in a twenty-four-hour vigilance task. All monitors were confined to the testing rooms for the whole period. The two-man teams were either allowed self-paced alternation, or given two hours on and two hours off duty. There was no statistical difference between the performance of these teams and that of individuals monitoring continuously for twenty-four hours. In each case there was a considerable deterioration in detections during the night hours. It was found that the best self-paced teams changed over less often than the worst teams. Little or no recovery was found over two hours' rest.

Other tasks

A number of authors have summarized work on the effects of rest pauses on performance in various tasks (see for instance, Adams, 1964; Poulton, 1966). Alluisi and Chiles (1967) studied the effect of various work-rest schedules on performance in a number of different tasks, such as vigilance and more active tasks. They reported that men could probably follow a schedule of four hours on duty and four hours off duty indefinitely. For shorter periods, such as a few weeks, they could work for four hours alternating with two hours off duty, without a reduction in performance.

The visual threshold for discrimination of luminance differences may deteriorate during a session, and be improved by rest pauses or between sessions (see J. F. Mackworth, 1969, chapter 2). McFarland *et al.* (1942) found that if the subject was allowed to move around for five minutes or so every half-hour, there was an improvement in visual sensitivity, though the threshold was not restored to the original level. If he were given the same rest period but required to fixate either a light or a dark patch without change in posture, no improvement occurred. It was found by Haider and Dixon (1961) that in the first session of testing the visual threshold there was no significant change, but there was a lowered threshold at the beginning of the second session. Increases in threshold were found during the second and later sessions. Thus, presumably the decrement (an intra-session increase in threshold) was masked in the first session by learning. The absolute auditory threshold was found by Zwislocki *et al.* (1958) to show an intra-session increase, with a decrease from session to session.

The effect of rest pauses in tracking tasks has been widely studied. Several studies have attempted to elucidate the cause of the improvement in performance that is found between the end of one trial and the beginning of the next, particularly in the pursuit-rotor task (reminiscence). Adams (1955) found that when the rest pause was occupied by visual pursuit activity there was no improvement. Humphries and McIntyre (1963a and b), however, found no effect of intervening activity upon reminiscence. A further study by Rosenquist (1965) examined the question of interpolated activity in detail. The subject was required to spend his rest period, between trials on the pursuit rotor, by watching the experimenter performing the same task; the subject had to press a button whenever the experimenter was off target. Reminiscence by these subjects was considerably less than that shown by subjects who did nothing during their rest period. If the period of watching was followed by a period of complete rest, then reminiscence followed the same course as it did during the complete rest alone. Time on target in the final trial increased with increasing duration of intervening rest, up to nine minutes. It would appear that the decrement (as revealed by reminiscence) was due to habituation to the sensory events of the task, since it did not dissipate when the subject was required to pay attention to the task, even though he was not actually doing the tracking himself.

Wilkinson (1959) used the 'five-choice serial reaction-time task' for testing subjects who had been deprived of sleep. Half the subjects received a thirty-second rest pause at the end of each five-minute period of work. This rest pause was announced by a bell, and ended by a warning light. In the control condition, the same signals were given but the subject was told to ignore them. It was found that at the end of twenty-five minutes of testing, the rate of correct response was greater with the breaks than without them. There was no interaction between the stresses of sleep loss and continuous performance. Even in the first five minutes of work, there was a difference between the level of performance with and without previous sleep. The rested subjects receiving breaks showed an improvement during the session, while the sleepless subjects in the continuous task showed a decrease in the rate of correct responses during the session. It would appear that with the rested subjects the unchanging level of performance during the continuous task concealed hidden learning and decrement.

Summary

There is a recovery in performance in a vigilance task between the end of one session and the beginning of the next. The over-all level of performance may decrease, increase or remain the same between sessions. Auditory tasks and visual tasks involving scanning have been particularly found to be performed better in successive sessions. False alarms have often been found to show a considerable reduction during the first few sessions and then stabilize at a very low level. This may be due to a change in criterion. Initially, subjects do not know how many signals to expect and may consequently give more false alarms than they do later in the session. An initial training session does not, however, abolish this change in a later session, so it may not be entirely due to a change in expectancy. Habituation of the evoked potential may give the same result.

Rest pauses of as little as five minutes have been shown to maintain performance. There does not seem to be any reason why such pauses should affect the criterion, and in an active tracking task the criterion is unlikely to be of importance. There is evidence that the decrement in the pursuit rotor may be related to habituation due to repetition of the visual stimuli. One of the characteristics of habituation is that it can be reversed by a very brief change in the rhythm of stimulation. Adding extra stimuli also produces dishabituation, and rest pauses usually involve extra stimuli to mark their onset, as well as whatever the subject pays attention to during the rest.

In conclusion, recovery of performance over short or long periods between testing is to be expected when the decrement in performance is due to inhibition, fatigue or habituation. It is less easy to explain the recovery in terms of expectancy.

8 Summary and Conclusions

When a human subject is required to detect and respond to a signal that has a low probability of occurrence during any one observation, there is a decrease in the probability of detection or the speed of response as the task continues. This decrease is defined as the vigilance decrement. There is also very likely to be a decrease in the proportion of false alarms, especially in the first session. The problem is to determine the nature and cause of these decrements. Explanations that have been offered include:

1. *Internal inhibition* due to monotony, leading to (a) habituation of the observing response; that is, decreases in the physiological responses to the recurrent events, particularly in the arousal responses of the brain; (b) habituation of the neural evoked responses, leading to changes in amplitude and pattern of these responses.

2. Changes in *expectancy* as the subject learns about the signal probability, leading to (a) changes in the observing rate, and (b) changes in the criterion of the subject.

A full discussion of the neural and physiological changes has been presented elsewhere (J. F. Mackworth, 1969). It was concluded that there is evidence of a decrease in arousal and of changes in the evoked potentials, but it is not yet fully proven that these changes are causally related to the vigilance decrement. The suggestion was made that as a result of a decrease in arousal, there would be an increase in the spontaneous neural noise, producing a decrease in sensitivity; drug data indicate that such a decrease in arousal may be accompanied by an increase in false alarms, or at least an absence of the usual decrease. On the other hand, a decrease in the amplitude of the potentials evoked by the background events of the task might result in an increase in sensitivity to the signal but a decrease in both correct detections and false alarms, because fewer events (signal or non-signal) will reach the predetermined criterial level. Thus these two changes, decreases in arousal level and in amplitude of the evoked potentials, might both lead to a decrease in detections, but tend to counteract each other in their effect on false alarms. False-alarm changes may be independent of changes in signal detections under certain circumstances, notably drugs and repeated sessions. There may be an improvement in detections between sessions, while false alarms may decrease between sessions, and stabilize at a very low level. In late sessions there may still be found a decrease in detections within a session, but no further change in false alarms. It is possible that the relative importance of the evoked potentials and the arousal response may change with repeated sessions; the habituation of the arousal response may become relatively more important in late sessions.

Vigilance as a Decision-Making Process

Decision theory presumes that the nature of a decision depends, among other factors, upon the rewards and punishments attached to correct and incorrect decisions. In the normal vigilance task there is no apparent result dependent upon the subject's decision, whether this is positive or negative. It has therefore been postulated that the decision process actually occurs at an earlier stage, when the subject decides whether or not to observe the display at any given moment. This *observing response* includes a whole series of changes, from neural to motor, and future research should be aimed at clarifying these changes. It is assumed that there is an increasingly heavy penalty attached to making an observation when no signal occurs, while the reward of detecting a signal is so rare that it plays little part in the decision. Why is it so difficult to pay attention to a monotonous display? The answer to this is tied in with the orienting response theory. The organism is so constructed that it pays maximum attention to the novel, unidentified and potentially dangerous event. In order to maintain this faculty of concentrated attention clear for such an event, it is necessary for the responses towards familiar, repetitive and unimportant stimuli to be repressed. It would appear that a stimulus is dealt with at two levels (at the very least). The first level accepts the stimulus, classifies it as unimportant or important, and represses it or passes it on to the higher level for attention. It can become almost impossible to maintain attention towards these suppressed events, as anyone knows who has struggled to pay attention to a lecturer who is giving vital information in a dull monotone.

Certain repetitive tasks may be acceptable just because they can be performed without attention. The well-learned programme of activity unrolls as if it were on tape while lively conversation or restless thoughts occupy the otherwise unused centre of the mental stage. In fact, the hands demand some activity, and those who are not encouraged by the social situation to make something, to knit or carve, may soothe this need by smoking or eating.

Such repetitive tasks often involve fairly complex movements, and the ability to perform these patterns of movement has the curious characteristic that it usually works best when attention is not paid to the actual movements. The typist who stops to think where her fingers should go often makes an error. On the other hand, the ability to make a fine perceptual discrimination involving considerable uncertainty appears to depend very closely upon the limelight of attention. In fact, the perception need not be so fine. Somewhere in the system is a decision-making process that is profoundly dependent on attention. The eye rests on the red traffic light, and no message of danger flashes from the preoccupied centre of attention to the muscles. Somehow, a connexion has not been made between the percept and the stored model. How the red light is selected from the multitude of visual stimuli being received concurrently is a process not as yet fully understood. The operator may be looking directly at the danger signal (as shown in eye movement studies, e.g. Mackworth, Kaplan and Metlay, 1964) and yet not know that he saw it. Sometimes one may stare at a wanted object for several seconds and suddenly recognize it. Perhaps we should wonder more at the speed of recognition of an object out of uncounted millions of objects that we could have recognized from stored information.

The *decision-making aspects* of the vigilance task are not easy to evaluate, because a number of assumptions have to be made which are of doubtful validity. The present state of knowledge is based on a number of approximations, using classic signal detection theory, and it is probable that further theoretical developments for applying the classical theory to such free response situations will have to be made. It would appear that the rate of background events is just as important, or even more so, than the signal rate, and that the probability that an event will be a signal is by no means the only causal relation with the probability of detection.

There are two main ways to calculate signal detection theory measures in a vigilance task. In one, the data consist simply of the number of correct and incorrect positive responses in a given period of time. Such a calculation allows the use of the classic vigilance task, with a simple push-button response when a signal is observed. It does, however, give estimates for d', the detectability of the signal, and *beta*, the criterion of the subject, which depend on the assumption of equal variances for signal and noise. Such an assumption is almost certainly untrue. The other method requires the subject to give an estimate of his level of certainty that he is correct, choosing one of two or more levels of certainty. Experiments using such a method have indicated that there may well be a change in the relative variances of the distributions of the 'noise' and the 'signal plus noise', during an experiment (especially in a visual task). At the beginning of the experiment, the signal-plus-noise distribution may have a considerably larger variance than that of the noise alone. Such a difference might arise when there was uncertainty about the nature of the

signal, or about its temporal distribution. This type of experiment is more revealing than the first type, but it is not
clear whether it entirely duplicates the classic vigilance task;
since such estimates of uncertainty by the subject might increase his level of arousal or the amplitude of the evoked
potential.

Experiments using these two methods have shown consistently that there is an increase in the strictness of the
criterion of the subject (*beta*) as the task proceeds, especially in
the initial session. The subject becomes less likely to give a
positive response, either correct or false, as the task proceeds.
Changes in the *detectability* of the signal during the task (*d'*)
have been found only in tasks with a continuous or very rapid
background event rate, or in late sessions.

There is evidence that the criterion of the subject is related
to the probability that an event will be a signal, especially
when the subjects have already had a training session. Once the
expectancy has been established there may still be a decrease in
detection during the session, with little or no change in false
alarms, indicating a decrease in signal detectability, without
any change in the criterion.

Sokolov (1963, p. 163) pointed out that the rate of habituation of the orienting response is reduced when the discrimination between signal and non-signal event becomes more
difficult. Measurements of detectability have confirmed this
finding in the few experiments in which two levels of signal
difficulty have been studied (J. F. Mackworth and Taylor,
1963). Table 2 (p. 44) also suggests that the changes in *d'* between pre-test and test were larger for the easier of two tasks.
With the visual task, in this experiment, changes in *beta* also
appeared to be larger for the easy task. It should be emphasized
that changes in detections may not show this effect (C. H. Baker,
1963a). Such changes are difficult to evaluate without concomitant records of false alarms.

Division of attention

The use of signal detectability measures has brought out an interesting difference between vigilance tasks and divided attention. While there is usually a *decrease* in false alarms during the vigilance task, there may actually be an *increase* when the task requires divided attention. Thus when the subject is required to attend to two or more tasks or channels simultaneously, there is a definite decrease in d', the detectability of the signal, in either channel. The data also suggest that the total detectability in the two channels together may be less than for either one when monitored alone. Thus the effort to divide the attention results in a loss of total channel capacity. The requirement to divide attention between two aspects of a task may also result in a reduced performance, as has been found when increased coding difficulty reduces the amount that can be memorized.

Observing responses

The use of signal detection theory has also emphasized the importance of the background event rate or the observing rate. It is assumed that the observer makes a decision about the presence of a signal every time he makes an observation of the display. Ideally, he should make an observation of each event, since each might be a signal; however, the observing response theory proposes that in fact the first level of decision is the decision whether or not to make an observation, and that this decision is made negatively more and more often as the task proceeds. (In other words, the observing responses habituate.) It is proposed that there is a considerable penalty attached to the observation of a non-signal event, and that this penalty increases as the task continues. The nature of the penalty is left vague, but it may be considered in neurological terms. Habituation of the observing response to repetitive events is 'built-in' genetically by evolutionary mechanisms, and to pay attention to a stimulus whose effect has habituated becomes increasingly difficult, as neural self-inhibition builds up. Thus the habituation hypothesis and the observing response hypothesis are almost identical.

The event rate

Both these hypotheses are based to a considerable extent on the finding of the importance of the event rate. To some extent, this finding is related to the probability that an event will be a signal. This probability can be reduced either by decreasing the number of signals in unit time, or increasing the number of non-signal events in unit time. There is some evidence that the ratio of signals to non-signal events is not the whole story, and that the background event rate may affect detections even when the signal–non-signal event ratio is kept constant; if the event rate is sufficiently slow, detections may remain high, even with a very low rate of signals. Under such circumstances, habituation of the observing response may be so slow as to be negligible.

It would appear that the number of false alarms in unit time depends more on the number of signals in unit time than on the probability that an event will be a signal. Thus, since the *d'* measure depends on the background event rate it tends to decrease and *beta* tends to increase with increasing event rates. *The fact that the false alarm rate is to some extent independent of the event rate throws some doubt on the assumptions of signal detection theory as applied to vigilance.*

Expectancy

It has been mentioned that the changes found during a vigilance task probably have two main interlocking causes. The first is the monotony of the task as a whole, and the second is the improbability of a signal. Decrements are found in active tracking tasks, in which a response is required at each moment, the direction and amplitude of the response being the major unknown factors (see J. F. Mackworth, 1969). If the task is still in process of being learnt, the decrement may appear as an improvement between one session and the next (reminiscence). Such a decrement in an active task would seem to be due mainly to habituation of the neural response to the repetitive series of events. But in a vigilance task there is added the temporal uncertainty of the signal. The majority of observing responses will be unrewarded by a signal, and hence the subject may decrease his observing rate as the task continues, because he learns about the low probability of the signal. The expectancy theory suggests that the subject observes the display when and where he expects from past evidence that a signal will occur. In general, the evidence suggests that the subject forms a minimum estimate of the probable interval between signals, and takes brief rests immediately after he has detected a signal. Thus signals that occur unexpectedly soon after a previous one tend to produce a less accurate response than other signals.

Such brief rests may produce dishabituation, and thus restore the level of performance. This may be one reason why vigilance performance tends to reach a steady level, as the subject reaches an equilibrium between the ability to predict the occurrence of a signal and the tendency to habituation of the unrewarded observing response.

It has been demonstrated that the criterion of the subject varies according to his training and experience of the task. Thus the subject is less likely to give false alarms in later sessions, so that the strictness of his criterial level (*beta*) rises even though he may detect as many signals in the later sessions, or even more, than in the first session. Thus there appears to be learning in the vigilance task, and some of the decrement within a task may be masked by this learning, just as learning is masked by a hidden decrement in more active tasks. Learning has been particularly demonstrated in auditory tasks. People in general may be less accustomed to detecting faint changes in auditory signals than in visual ones.

While the formation of expectancies or models of the temporal aspects of the task may be part of the cause of the decrement, there still remains the problem of why subjects begin each session at the same (or higher) level as they began the first. It has been shown that subjects do carry over expectancies from one session to the next, so it would seem that some other explanation is necessary in addition to the expectancy hypothesis. Dishabituation of the neural responses to the events of the task might be expected to occur between each session, especially of the arousal responses, and therefore habituation would be seen within each session.

In addition to the relation between over-all signal probability and performance, there is also a relation between the regularity of the signal interval and performance. It is clear that with more regular intervals the ability to make an observing response at the right moment when a signal occurs will improve. The relation between signal interval and performance is, however, complex. It is possible that when the shortest interval is very brief, fifteen seconds or so, better performance may be found following this shortest interval, due perhaps to the occurrence of the signal within the period of arousal or dishabituation produced by the last signal. With somewhat longer minimum intervals, performance tends to improve as the signal interval approaches the mean.

The relation between the event rate and S D T measures

The level of expectancy for a signal will depend on both the absolute signal rate in real time, and also on the relative signal–non-signal event ratio. The effect of varying the signal rate, when the event rate is kept constant, is somewhat variable, though in general the probability that a signal will be detected improves as the signal rate increases. The effect of the background rate, however, appears to be considerably larger and more consistent, though it has received less study as yet. Because the percentage of false alarms is the ratio of false positive responses to the event rate, the relation between the probability of detection and the event rate is not necessarily reflected by changes in d'. There may however be considerable differences in the criterial level (*beta*), though it may be observed that if there were no change in the absolute number of signals detected nor in the absolute number of false alarms there would appear to be a large increase in *beta* when the event rate was increased. Since it appears probable that the false alarm rate, in absolute time, is more dependent on the signal rate than on the event rate, it is doubtful whether this apparent increase in *beta* really represents any change in the subject's criterion.

Experiments have suggested that changes in the detectability of the signal are only found in tasks in which the event rate is very high or continuous, although such changes may appear when the subject is fully familiar with the task. Changes in *beta* during the task are most marked during the first session, or when a training session is followed by one with a different probability of signal occurrence; these changes are very likely to represent the formation of or change in expectancies, though they may also be related to habituation of the neural evoked responses to the events of the task.

Knowledge of results

Any stimulus which conveys information to the subject about the task and his performance may improve the level of performance and reduce the decrement. The effect of feedback in maintaining and sometimes improving performance in a vigilance task is a fairly consistent finding, though there are exceptions. Improvement may occur even when feedback is related to only a few of the signals, or is given on an auxiliary task. The mechanism of the effect is complex, and only direct neurological experiments can be expected to disentangle the various aspects. It appears that knowledge of results can alter the criterion, and can increase the detectability of the signal for the subject.

There is often a higher probability of signal detection right from the beginning of the task with knowledge of results; by the end of the task there may be marked differences between control and knowledge of results sessions for all four statistics, i.e. signal detection probability, false alarm probability, d', and *beta*. These differences may extend to a second session without knowledge of results which may also maintain the speed of response in a task in which all or nearly all the signals

are detected. It has also been found that the effects of knowledge of results and the stimulant drug amphetamine are
additive. Both will maintain the level of performance separately, and together they may produce an actual improvement
during the session.

The effect of knowledge of results depends on the nature
of the response that is reinforced. Differences may be found
when only missed signals are 'punished' by feedback, as
compared with the task in which false alarms are also indicated. If feedback is given only following false alarms, there
may be an exaggeration of the usual increase in caution. The
informative or motivating effects of feedback are an essential
aspect of its effect on performance.

The motivating or arousing effects of feedback may also be
demonstrated by the use of false information. Such random
feedback may also produce an improvement in detections, if
the subject believes that this feedback is related to his performance. There may, however, be some differences between
the effect of true and false knowledge of results. The rate of
decrement may be greater with false knowledge than with
true; while true feedback following missed or all signals allows
the subject to make accurate estimates of the probability of a
signal, false information does not.

Motivation

Motivating factors may affect either of the two decision levels
discussed, previously: the decision to observe the display and
the decision to give a positive response. Such extra factors may
also affect the levels of arousal directly. Duffy (1962, p. 9)
pointed out that 'situations having a high degree of significance will . . . produce a high degree of activation'. Motivation
may be increased by offering rewards, by public display of the
scores, by telling subjects that they are going to be given
information about their performance on a secondary task, or
in many other ways. None of these methods necessarily gives
extra stimulation during the task yet they may result in improved performance. Such increased motivation may affect not

merely the criterion but also the sensitivity of the subject for a signal. It has been mentioned that increased arousal or the orienting response may increase sensitivity in a number of ways, both peripheral and central. It is possible that there may also be an indirect relation between motivation and arousal, in that subjects may attempt to maintain their level of vigilance by bodily movements, as well as by making more observing responses.

The knowledge that the end of a session is approaching improves performance, and better detection may be found when the session is known to be a short one. Sokolov (1963) found that habituation was delayed when the discrimination was more difficult, and McGrath (1965) suggested that subjects were more highly aroused when the signal was more difficult to detect. Such findings may also be related to motivation.

Recovery between testing

Rest pauses of half-an-hour or longer have generally proved adequate for complete restoration of performance (see chapter 7). Even an expected rest pause of quite short duration, such as thirty seconds each half-hour, can produce marked improvement in performance. There is clearly some motivating effect here. Such rest pauses are often accompanied by novel stimuli, such as bells or movements, which indicate their occurrence and occupy the pause. There does not seem to be any reason why rest pauses should alter the expectancy of the subject. On the other hand, any slight change in the steady sequence of events may produce dishabituation, especially of the evoked potential responses to these recurrent events. When there is a continuous background movement, as with the Continuous Clock Test, short rest pauses up to ten minutes combined with disappearance of the display may not improve performance. Even when a new version of the task is introduced every ten minutes, there may not be complete recovery. It has been suggested that in this task, in which there are no discrete background events, and decrements in d' have been consistently found, that changes in arousal (related to the over-all environment as well as to the task) may be more important than changes in the evoked potential.

It is interesting to note that rest pauses between sessions may restore detections to their original level, but may not restore false alarms. Thus changes in false alarms may well be related to changes in expectancy, since models of the temporal pattern of signals will probably be carried over from one session to the next. It has been suggested that reductions in evoked potentials may lead to a decrease in both false alarms and detections, resulting in an increase in *beta*. Such changes are maximal in early sessions, while in later sessions changes in d' may be observed.

General Conclusions

Decrements in performance may be observed during a monotonous task, even when continuous responses are required. Such changes may be related to reductions in the observing responses, if these are interpreted as neural. Reductions in the arousal or orienting response can be expected as a result of repetitive patterns of stimuli. Stimulant drugs can prevent such decrements in performance. The performance changes may also be related to habituation of the neural responses evoked by the monotonous events. In a vigilance task the factor of expectancy is probably important. The subjects may be less willing to make an observing response, and also less willing to give a positive response to an event, as they realize that the probability that an event will be a signal is low. Thus the decline in both correct and incorrect positive responses during a vigilance task may be due both to an increased unwillingness to respond positively, that is, a real *change in criterion*, and also to habituation of the evoked neural responses, which may result in fewer events, either signal or nonsignal, reaching the previously established criterial level. Reductions in the orienting response may lead to a *decreased sensitivity* to the signal, which may become visible in later sessions, or when the background event rate is very rapid or continuous.

These suggestions are put forward in the hope that they will be tested in further experiments. The broad outline of the vigilance field and its relation to physiological data that has been brought together in this and the previous volume (J. F. Mackworth, 1969) should make it easier for workers to define such experiments. It is also hoped that physiologists may find in these pages data that will interest them sufficiently to work towards narrowing the gap that too often exists between the two closely dependent sciences of psychology and neurophysiology. While the relation between mind and matter is still an unresolved problem, it is certain that the mind has great difficulty in communicating with other minds without the intervention of the brain and body. Equally, the brain and body have very little normal function without the mind exercising its control through them.

Appendix

Types of Vigilance Tasks

The vigilance task was designed to measure a hypothetical state of vigilance, which was defined as 'a state of readiness to detect and respond to certain specified small changes occurring at random time intervals in the environment' (N. H. Mackworth, 1957, p. 389). The essence of the task is, therefore, the temporal uncertainty of the signals. In the majority of vigilance tasks, the probability that there will be a signal at any particular moment is extremely low. The response is usually a simple requirement to indicate when a signal has occurred. The effect of presenting more than one kind of signal and requiring more than one kind of response has also been studied.

Vigilance tasks can be grouped under two major headings – tasks in which the important measure of performance is the probability of signal detection, and tasks in which the important measure is the latency of response. Tasks measuring the effective threshold are a combination of these two measures. More recently, the importance of the false alarm has also been realized (see chapter 2 above). The term 'decrement' is used to indicate a decrease in performance between the beginning and end of the session.

Since almost every experiment has presented a slightly different task, the following examples are only representative. Many others will be found in the book. The following classification is necessarily somewhat arbitrary:

I. One Kind of Signal and One Kind of Response

1. Single signal source

    A. Dependent variable: probability of signal detection.
            (i) Visual tasks.
           (ii) Auditory tasks.
        (iii) Cutaneous stimuli.
    B. Dependent variable: reaction time.
            (i) Visual tasks.
           (ii) Auditory tasks.
    C. Dependent variable: effective threshold.
            (i) Visual tasks.
           (ii) Auditory tasks.

2. Multiple signal sources (visual tasks)

II. More than One Kind of Signal

III. More than One Kind of Response

I. One Kind of Signal and One Kind of Response

1. Single signal source

A. Dependent variable: probability of signal detection

(i) Visual tasks

a. The Clock Test (N. H. Mackworth, 1950).
b. The signal was a dim light appearing against a blank background. Known signal location (Adams, 1956; Teichner, 1962). Variable signal location (C. H. Baker, 1960b; Wilkinson, 1960).
c. The addition of a rotating sweep hand simulated a radar task (N. H. Mackworth, 1950; C. H. Baker, 1958; Wallis and Samuel, 1961).
d. The signal was a brief pause in a continuous light (R. A. Baker, Ware and Sipowicz, 1962b).
e. The signal was a brief pause in a rotating second hand of a clock (Continuous Clock, C. H. Baker, 1962b).

f. Twenty lights arranged in a circle were lit in rotation at 12 r.p.m. The signal was a missing light (Bergum and Lehr, 1962a).

g. The signal was a brighter pulse in a train of one-second light pulses occurring once every three seconds (Buckner and McGrath, 1963a).

h. The signal was an increased deflection of the pointer on a voltmeter. The non-signal events were either regular deflections once a second (Jenkins, 1958) or continuous oscillation (C. H. Baker, 1963b).

i. Two recent tasks have used an oscilloscope. In one, the events were a series of double movements of a bar of light. The signal was a larger movement of one member of the pair (Jerison and Pickett, 1964). In the other, the signal was an irregular vertical deflection of a horizontal trace moving across the face of the scope once every six seconds (Johnson and Payne, 1966).

j. The event was a strip of six discs, and the signal was either a black dot on a disc, a larger disc or a paler green disc (Colquhoun, 1959, 1961; Colquhoun and Baddeley, 1964).

k. The events were a series of random digits, presented one a second, and the signal was an odd-even-odd series (Corcoran, 1962).

(ii) Auditory tasks

a. The majority of auditory tasks have presented a series of tones or pulses of noise. In the Mackworth Listening Task, the two-second tones occurred at a rate of about three per minute, and the signal was a longer tone (N. H. Mackworth, 1950). Signals have been louder (Buckner and McGrath, 1963a; Binford and Loeb, 1963), softer (Wilkinson, Morlock and Williams, 1966), different frequency (Floyd, Griggs and R. A. Baker, 1961), or a longer interval between tones (Alluisi and Hall, 1963).

b. The signal was a brief tone against a blank background (Loeb and Schmidt, 1963); or a brief interruption of a continuous tone (Ware, 1961).

c. The signal was a series of odd-even-odd digits in a continuous set of random digits (Bakan, 1961).

d. Poulton (1960) presented strings of eight digits. The signal was a change of one number to a six between one string and the next.

(*iii*) *Cutaneous stimuli*

a. Decrements in detection of cutaneous signals, whether presented as occasional signals against a blank background, or as longer signals in a series, have been reported (Hawkes and Loeb, 1961, 1962; Loeb and Hawkes, 1961, 1962).

B. Dependent variable: reaction time

It has been found that reaction time to a simple signal increased during the session in the following representative experiments (see Buck, 1966).

(*i*) *Visual tasks*

a. The signal was a light appearing against a blank background (McCormack, 1958).

b. Increases in R T have also been found in simulated radar (Wallis and Samuel, 1961).

c. The signal was a change of a symbol from G to F (Adams and Boulter, 1962).

d. The signal was a deflection of a horizontal sweep (Halcomb and Kirk, 1965).

(*ii*) *Auditory tasks*

a. The signal was a 0·6-second tone against a blank background (Loeb and Schmidt, 1963).

b. A pulse of higher frequency in a series of five-second pulses (Dardano, 1965).

c. A change in frequency of a continuous tone (Webb and Wherry, 1960).

C. Dependent variable: effective threshold

In the following experiments, the signal was repeated in

increasing steps of brightness or loudness until detected. An increase in the intensity required for response occurred during the session.

(i) Visual tasks

a. The signal was an increasing brightness of a steady spot of light (Kirk, 1962).
b. Bakan (1955) presented two lights simultaneously. The signal was an increase in brightness of one of the lights.
c. The signal was a brighter flash in a train of flashes occurring once a second. The signal was repeated every five seconds at a brighter level until detected (Zuercher, 1965).

(ii) Auditory tasks

a. A tone pulse was presented against a noisy background every thirty seconds at increasing intensity until detected (Elliott, 1957).
b. The signal was an increased intensity of the second number of a pair of pulses (Gettys, 1964).

2. Multiple signal sources (visual tasks)

It has been suggested (Broadbent, 1958) that a decrement may fail to occur in tasks employing multiple sources, because shifting attention from one source to another may prevent the changes which normally give rise to the decrement.

a. Dials. Garvey, Taylor and Newlin (1959) presented eight dials with randomly dithering pointers. The signal was an increased deflection into a marked area. There was an increase in R T and in the percentage of signals missed as the run continued. Wiener (1964b) used one to three volt-meters, and found that the number of sources had no effect on the decrement in detection of an increased deflection. Howland and Wiener (1963) found no decrements in detections in a similar task with four voltmeters, but there was a marked increase in false alarms during the session.
b. Adams and Boulter (1964) presented a signal that was a two-digit number appearing at one of three sources. The

increase in R T during the session was not significant. Luce
(1964) presented a signal at one of five different sources.
There was an increase in R T during the session, but when
the signal could have been one of seven different symbols,
R T was high but did not increase during the session.

c. Broadbent (1958) found no change in R T during the
session when the signal could appear on any of twenty
dials.

d. Jerison (1963) used three Jump Clocks, and found no
decrement in the very low level of detections.

e. Broadbent and Gregory (1963b) found no changes in
detections during the session in a task presenting three
lights flashing simultaneously.

f. Howell, Johnston and Goldstein (1966) examined a task in
which alpha numeric stimuli appeared in sixty-four possible
locations on an 8×8 matrix. The signal was a change in
the display. Maximum increases in latency during the
session were found with low frequency of signal, and high
density of stimuli.

II. More than One Kind of Signal

a. Hatfield and Loeb (1968) compared detection of one intensity of signal with detection of three intensities, and
found that there was a significant decrease in detections
and false alarms with both conditions. They used both
visual and auditory tasks. Reaction times increased
during the session. There were significant declines in
sensitivity (d') with one signal intensity, but not with
three intensities.

b. O'Hanlon, Schmidt and C. H. Baker (1965) presented three
kinds of signals in a sonar task. No decline in detections
was found during the session, but there was a decline in
false alarms, suggesting an increase in sensitivity.

c. Levine (1966) presented three kinds of auditory signals, of
differing frequency, but subjects expected five kinds.
There were five response switches for the five kinds of

signal, and three switches for degrees of confidence. Decreases in detections and in false alarms were found. There were increases in *beta*, but no change in sensitivity (d') during the session.

d. Kidd and Micocci (1964) used a task in which the events were a series of stock market quotations. Subjects had to identify one to three firms as signals. More signals were missed as the number of kinds of signals increased.

III. More than One Kind of Response

a. Adams, Stenson and Humes (1961) compared simple detection with four-choice evaluation. Latencies were much longer for evaluation, but no increase occurred during the session, in contrast to the simple detection. Luce (1964) found that adding a memory requirement to detection increased latency, but there was no further increase during the session. (See also Monty, 1962.)

b. A number of workers have applied signal detection theory to vigilance tasks by requiring the subject to grade the confidence of his response. Broadbent and Gregory (1963b) required a simple response, followed by an indication of the confidence level. In a visual task, Broadbent and Gregory (1965) required subjects to press one of three buttons after every flash. Loeb and Binford (1964) used three buttons, one of which was to be pressed when the subject thought there had been a signal. All these workers found a decrease in the number of 'sure' responses during a session, and an increase in criterial level (*beta*).

References

ADAMS, J. A. (1955), 'A source of decrement in psychomotor performance', *J. exp. Psychol.*, vol. 49, pp. 390–94.

ADAMS, J. A. (1956), 'Vigilance in the detection of low-intensity visual stimuli', *J. exp. Psychol.*, vol. 52, pp. 204–8.

ADAMS, J. A. (1964), 'Motor skills', *Ann. Rev. Psychol.*, vol. 64, pp. 495–504.

ADAMS, J. A., and BOULTER, L. R. (1962), 'An evaluation of the activationist hypothesis of human vigilance', *J. exp. Psychol.*, vol. 64, pp. 495–504.

ADAMS, J. A., and BOULTER, L. R. (1964), 'Spatial and temporal uncertainty as determinants of vigilance behavior', *J. exp. Psychol.*, vol. 67, pp. 127–31.

ADAMS, J. A., and HUMES, J. M. (1963), 'Monitoring of complex visual displays: IV. Training for vigilance', *Human Factors*, vol. 5, pp. 147–53.

ADAMS, J. A., HUMES, J. M., and STENSON, H. H. (1962), 'Monitoring of complex visual displays: III. Effects of repeated sessions on human vigilance', *Human Factors*, vol. 4, pp. 149–57.

ADAMS, J. A., HUMES, J. M., and SIEVEKING, N. A. (1963), 'Monitoring of complex visual displays: V. Effects of repeated sessions, and heavy visual load on human vigilance', *Human Factors*, vol. 5, pp. 385–9.

ADAMS, J. A., STENSON, H. H., and HUMES, J. M. (1961), 'Monitoring of complex visual displays: II. Effects of visual load and response complexity on human vigilance', *Human Factors*, vol. 3, pp. 213–21.

ALLUISI, E. A., and CHILES, W. D. (1967), 'Sustained performance, work–rest scheduling, and diurnal rhythms in man', *Acta Psychologica*, vol. 27, pp. 436–42.

ALLUISI, E. A., and HALL, T. J. (1963), 'Declines in auditory vigilance during periods of high multiple-task activity', *Percept. mot. Skills*, vol. 16, pp. 739–74.

ANTROBUS, J. S., and SINGER, J. L. (1964), 'Visual signal detection as a function of sequential variability of simultaneous speech', *J. exp. Psychol.*, vol. 68, pp. 603–10.

BAKAN, P. (1955), 'Discrimination decrement as a function of time on a prolonged vigil', *J. exp. Psychol.*, vol. 50, pp. 387–9.

BAKAN, P. (1961), 'Effect of meprobamate on auditory vigilance', *Percept. mot. Skills*, vol. 12, p. 26.

BAKAN, P., and MANLEY, R. (1963), 'Effect of visual deprivation on auditory vigilance', *Brit. J. Psychol.*, vol. 54, pp. 114–19.

BAKER, C. H. (1958), 'Attention to visual displays during a vigilance task. I. Biassing attention', *Brit. J. Psychol.*, vol. 49, pp. 279–88.

BAKER, C. H. (1959a), 'Attention to visual displays during a vigilance task. II. Maintaining the level of vigilance', *Brit. J. Psychol.*, vol. 50, pp. 30–36.

BAKER, C. H. (1959b), 'Towards a theory of vigilance', *Canad. J. Psychol.*, vol. 13, pp. 35–42.

BAKER, C. H. (1960a), 'Observing behavior in a vigilance task', *Science*, vol. 132, pp. 674–5.

BAKER, C. H. (1960b), 'Maintaining the level of vigilance by means of artificial signals', *J. appl. Psychol.*, vol. 44, pp. 336–8.

BAKER, C. H. (1961), 'Maintaining the level of vigilance by means of knowledge of results about a secondary vigilance task', *Ergonomics*, vol. 4, pp. 311–16.

BAKER, C. H. (1962a), 'On temporal extrapolation', *Canad. J. Psychol.*, vol. 16, pp. 37–41.

BAKER, C. H. (1962b), 'Probability of signal detection in a vigilance task', *Science*, vol. 136, p. 46.

BAKER, C. H. (1963a), 'Signal duration as a factor in vigilance tasks', *Science*, vol. 141, pp. 1196–7.

BAKER, C. H. (1963b), 'Consistency of performance in two visual vigilance tasks', in Buckner, D. N., and McGrath, J. J. (eds.), *Vigilance: A Symposium*, McGraw-Hill, pp. 43–50.

BAKER, C. H. (1963c), 'Further towards a theory of vigilance', in Buckner, D. N., and McGrath, J. J. (eds.), *Vigilance: A Symposium*, McGraw-Hill, pp. 127–53.

BAKER, C. H., and HARABEDIAN, A. (1962), 'Performance in an auditory vigilance task while simultaneously tracking a visual target', *Technical Report*, no. 740–42, Human Factors Research, Inc.

BAKER, R. A., SIPOWICZ, R. R., and WARE, J. R. (1961), 'Effects of practice on visual monitoring', *Percept. mot. Skills*, vol. 13, pp. 291–4.

BAKER, R. A., WARE, J. R., and SIPOWICZ, R. R. (1962a), 'Vigilance: a comparison in auditory, visual and combined audio-visual tasks', *Canad. J. Psychol.*, vol. 16, pp. 192–8.

BAKER, R. A., WARE, J. R., and SIPOWICZ, R. R. (1962b), 'Sustained vigilance: I. Signal detection during a twenty-four hour continuous watch', *Psychol. Record*, vol. 12, 245–50.

BERGUM, B. O., and LEHR, D. J. (1962a), 'Vigilance performance as a function of interpolated rest', *J. appl. Psychol.*, vol. 46, pp. 425–7.

BERGUM, B. O., and LEHR, D. J. (1962b), 'Vigilance performance as a function of paired monitoring', *J. appl. Psychol.*, vol. 46, pp. 341–3.

BERGUM, B. O., and LEHR, D. J. (1963a), 'End spurt in vigilance', *J. exp. Psychol.*, vol. 66, pp. 383–5.

BERGUM, B. O., and LEHR, D. J. (1963b), 'Effects of authoritarianism on vigilance performance', *J. appl. Psychol.*, vol. 47, pp. 75–7.

BERGUM, B. O., and LEHR, D. J. (1963c), 'Vigilance performance as a function of task and environmental variables', HumRRO Report Section 11, U.S. Army Air Defense Human Research Unit.

BERGUM, B. O., and LEHR, D. J. (1964), 'Monetary incentives and vigilance', *J. exp. Psychol.*, vol. 67, pp. 197–8.

BEVAN, W., AVANT, L. L., and LANKFORD, H. G. (1966), 'Serial reaction time and the temporal pattern of prior signals', *Amer. J. Psychol.*, vol. 79, pp. 551–9.

BEVAN, W., AVANT, L., and LANKFORD, H. A. (1967), 'Influence of interpolated periods of activity and inactivity upon the vigilance decrement', *J. appl. Psychol.*, vol. 51, pp. 352–6.

BEVAN, W., HARDESTY, D. L., and AVANT, U. L. (1965), 'Response latency with constant and variable interval schedules', *Percept. mot. Skills.*, vol. 20, pp. 969–72.

BEVAN, W., and TURNER, E. D. (1965), 'Vigilance performance with a qualitative shift in verbal reinforcers', *J. exp. Psychol.*, vol. 70, pp. 83–6.

BINFORD, J. R., and LOEB, M. (1963), 'Monitoring readily detected auditory signals and detection of obscure visual signals', *Percept. mot. Skills*, vol. 17, pp. 735–46.

BINFORD, J. R., and LOEB, M. (1966), 'Changes within and over repeated sessions in criterion and effective sensitivity in an auditory vigilance task', *J. exp. Psychol.*, vol. 72, pp. 339–45.

BLAIR, W. C. (1958), 'Measurement of observing responses in human monitoring', *Science*, vol. 128, pp. 255–6.

BOULTER, L. R., and ADAMS, J. A. (1963), 'Vigilance decrement, the expectancy hypothesis and intersignal interval', *Canad. J. Psychol.*, vol. 17, pp. 201–9.

BOWEN, H. M. (1964), 'Vigilance as a function of signal frequency and flash rate', *Percept. mot. Skills*, vol. 18, pp. 333–8.

BROADBENT, D. E. (1958), *Perception and Communication*, Pergamon Press.

BROADBENT, D. E. (1963a), 'Some recent research from the Applied Psychology Research Unit, Cambridge', in Buckner, D. N., and

McGrath, J. J. (eds.), *Vigilance: A Symposium*, McGraw-Hill, pp. 72–82.

BROADBENT, D. E., and GREGORY, M. (1963a), 'Division of attention and the decision theory of signal detection', *Proc. Roy. Soc., B.*, vol. 158, pp. 222–31.

BROADBENT, D. E., and GREGORY, M. (1963b), 'Vigilance considered as a statistical decision', *Brit. J. Psychol.*, vol. 54, pp. 309–23.

BROADBENT, D. E., and GREGORY, M. (1965), 'Effects of noise and of signal rate upon vigilance analysed by means of decision theory', *Human Factors*, vol. 7, pp. 155–62.

BUCK, L. (1966), 'Reaction time as a measure of perceptual vigilance', *Psychol. Bull.*, vol. 65, pp. 291–304.

BUCKNER, D. N., HARABEDIAN, A., and McGRATH, J. J. (1960), 'A study of individual differences in vigilance performance', *Technical Report*, no. 2, Human Factors Research, Inc.

BUCKNER, D. N., HARABEDIAN, A., and McGRATH, J. J. (1965), 'Individual differences in vigilance performance', *J. engin. Psychol.*, vol. 4, pp. 69–85.

BUCKNER, D. N., and McGRATH, J. J. (1963a), 'A comparison of performances on single and dual sensory mode vigilance tasks', in Buckner, D. N., and McGrath, J. J. (eds.), *Vigilance: A Symposium*, McGraw-Hill, pp. 53–69.

BUCKNER, D. N., and McGRATH, J. J. (eds.), (1963b), *Vigilance: A Symposium*, McGraw-Hill.

CHINN, McC. R., and ALLUISI, E. A. (1964), 'Effect of three kinds of knowledge of results on three measures of vigilance performance', *Percept. mot. Skills*, vol. 18, pp. 901–12.

COLQUHOUN, W. P. (1959), 'The effect of a short rest pause on inspection efficiency', *Ergonomics*, vol. 2, pp. 367–72.

COLQUHOUN, W. P. (1961), 'The effect of "unwanted" signals on performance in a vigilance task', *Ergonomics*, vol. 4, pp. 41–51.

COLQUHOUN, W. P. (1966a), 'Training for vigilance: a comparison of different techniques', *Human Factors*, vol. 8, pp. 7–12.

COLQUHOUN, W. P. (1966b), 'The effect of "unwanted" signals on performance in a vigilance task; a reply to Jerison', *Ergonomics*, vol. 9, pp. 417–19.

COLQUHOUN, W. P., and BADDELEY, A. D. (1964), 'Role of pre-test expectancy in vigilance decrement', *J. exp. Psychol.*, vol. 68, pp. 156–60.

COLQUHOUN, W. P., and BADDELEY, A. D. (1967), 'The influence of signal probability during pretraining on vigilance decrement', *J. exp. Psychol.*, vol. 73, pp. 153–4.

CORCORAN, D. W. J. (1962), 'Noise and loss of sleep', *Quart. J. exp. Psychol.*, vol. 14, pp. 178–82.

DARDANO, J. F. (1962), 'Relationship of intermittent noise, intersignal interval, and skin conductance to vigilance behavior', *J. app. Psychol.*, vol. 46, pp. 106–14.

DARDANO, J. F. (1965), 'Modification of observing behavior', *J. exp. anal. Behav.*, vol. 8, pp. 207–14.

DAVIES, D. R., and HOCKEY, G. R. J. (1966), 'The effects of noise and doubling the signal frequency on individual differences in visual vigilance performance', *Brit. J. Psychol.*, vol. 57, pp. 381–9.

DEESE, J. (1955), 'Some problems in the theory of vigilance', *Psychol. Rev.*, vol. 62, pp. 359–86.

DE LORGE, J. O., HESS, J., and CLARK, F. C. (1967), 'Observing behavior in the squirrel monkey in a situation analogous to human monitoring', *Percept. mot. Skills*, vol. 25, pp. 745–67.

DONCHIN, E., and LINDSLEY, D. B. (1966), 'Average evoked potential and reaction time to visual stimuli', *Electroenceph. clin. Neurophysiol.*, vol. 20, pp. 217–23.

DUFFY, E. (1962), *Activation and Behavior*, Wiley.

EASON, R. G., ODEN, D., and WHITE, C. T. (1967), 'Visually evoked cortical potentials and reaction time in relation to site of retinal stimulation', *Electroenceph. clin. Neurophysiol.*, vol. 23, pp. 213–24.

EDWARDS, W., LINDMAN, H., and PHILLIPS, L. D. (1965), 'Emerging techniques for making decisions', in Newcomb, T. M. (ed.), *New Directions in Psychology II*, Holt, Rinehart & Winston, pp. 259–325.

EGAN, J. P., GREENBERG, G. Z., and SCHULMAN, A. I. (1961a), 'Interval of time uncertainty in auditory detection', *J. Acoust. Soc. Amer.*, vol. 33, pp. 771–8.

EGAN, J. P., GREENBERG, G. Z., and SCHULMAN, A. I. (1961b), 'Operating characteristics, signal detectability and the method of free response', *J. Acoust. Soc. Amer.*, vol. 33, pp. 993–1007.

EGAN, J. P., SCHULMAN, A. I., and GREENBERG, G. Z. (1961), 'Memory for waveform and time uncertainty in auditory detection', *J. Acoust. Soc. Amer.*, vol. 33, pp. 779–81.

ELLIS, H. C., and AHR, A. E. (1960), 'The role of error density and set in a vigilance task', *J. appl. Psychol.*, vol. 44, pp. 205–9.

ELLIOTT, E. (1957), 'Auditory vigilance tasks', *Advancement of Science*, no. 53, pp. 393–9.

ELLIOTT, E. (1960), 'Perception and alertness', *Ergonomics*, vol. 3, pp. 357–64.

EYSENCK, H. J., and THOMPSON, W. (1966), 'The effect of distraction on pursuit rotor learning, performance and reminiscence', *Brit. J. Psychol.*, vol. 57, pp. 99–106.

FAULKNER, T. W. (1962), 'Variability of detection in a vigilance task', *J. appl. Psychol.*, vol. 46, pp. 325–8.

FLOYD, A., GRIGGS, G. D., and BAKER, R. A. (1961), 'Role of expectancy in auditory vigilance', *Percept. mot. Skills*, vol. 13, pp. 131–4.

FREEMAN, G. L. (1940), 'The relation between performance and bodily activity level', *J. exp. Psychol.*, vol. 26, pp. 602–8.

FREEMAN, P. R. (1964), 'Table of d' and beta', Medical Research Council, *A.P.U. Report*, 529/64.

GARVEY, W. D., TAYLOR, F. V., and NEWLIN, E. P. (1959), 'The use of "artificial signals" to enhance monitoring performance', *N.R.L. Report*, 5269.

GETTYS, C. (1964), 'The alerted effective threshold in an auditory vigilance task', *J. aud. Res.*, vol. 4, pp. 23–38.

GLUCKSBERG, S. (1963), 'Rotary pursuit tracking with divided attention to cutaneous, visual and auditory signals', *J. engin. Psychol.*, vol. 2, pp. 119–25.

GOULD, J. D., and SCHAFFER, A. (1967), 'The effects of divided attention on visual monitoring of multi-channel displays', *Human Factors*, vol. 9, pp. 191–202.

GREEN, D. M., and SWETS, J. A. (1966), *Signal Detection Theory and Psychophysics*, Wiley.

HACK, J. M., ROBINSON, H. W., and LATHROP, R. G. (1965), 'Auditory distraction and compensatory tracking', *Percept. mot. Skills*, vol. 20, pp. 228–30.

HAIDER, M. (1967), 'Vigilance, attention, expectation and cortical evoked potentials', in Sanders, A. F. (ed.), *Attention and Performance, Acta Psychologica*, vol. 27, pp. 246–52, North-Holland Publishing Co.

HAIDER, M., and DIXON, N. F. (1961), 'Influence of training and fatigue on the continuous recording of a visual differential threshold', *Brit. J. Psychol.*, vol. 52, pp. 227–37.

HAIDER, M., SPONG, P., and LINDSLEY, D. B. (1964), 'Attention, vigilance and cortical evoked potential in humans', *Science*, vol. 145, pp. 180–81.

HALCOMB, C. G., and KIRK, R. E. (1965), 'Organismic variables as predictors of vigilance behavior', *Percept. mot. Skills*, vol. 21, pp. 547–52.

HARDESTY, D., and BEVAN, W. (1964), 'Forms of orally-presented KR and serial reaction time', *Psychol. Rev.*, vol. 14, pp. 445–8.

HARDESTY, D., and BEVAN, W. (1965), 'Response latency as a function of the temporal pattern of stimulation', *Psychol. Rev.*, vol. 15, pp. 385–92.

HARDESTY, D., TRUMBO, D., and BEVAN, W. (1963), 'Influence of knowledge of results on performance in a monitoring task', *Percept. mot. Skills*, vol. 16, p. 629.

HARMON, F. L. (1933), 'The effects of noise upon certain psychological and physiological processes', *Arch. Psychol.*, no. 147.

HATFIELD, J. L., and LOEB, M. (1968), 'Sense mode and coupling in a vigilance task', *Percept. Psychophys.*, vol. 4, pp. 29–36.

HAUTY, G. T., and PAYNE, R. B. (1955), 'Mitigation of work decrement', *J. exp. Psychol.*, vol. 49, pp. 60–67.

HAWKES, G. R., and LOEB, M. (1961), 'Vigilance for cutaneous and auditory signals', *J. aud. Research*, vol. 4, pp. 272–84.

HAWKES, G. R., and LOEB, M. (1962), 'Vigilance for cutaneous and auditory stimuli as a function of intersignal interval and signal strength', *J. Psychol.*, vol. 53, pp. 211–18.

HEBB, D. O. (1969), 'The mind's eye', *Psychology Today*, vol. 2, no. 12, pp. 54–8.

HERNÁNDEZ-PEÓN, R., and STERMAN, M. B. (1966), 'Brain functions', *Ann. Rev. Psychol.*, vol. 17, pp. 363–94.

HOLLAND, J. G. (1957), 'Technique for behavioral analysis of human observing', *Science*, vol. 125, pp. 348–50.

HOLLAND, J. G. (1963), 'Human vigilance', *Science*, 1958, vol. 128, pp. 61–7; reprinted in Buckner, D. N., and McGrath, J. J. (eds.), *Vigilance: A Symposium*, McGraw-Hill.

HOWELL, W. C., JOHNSTON, W. A., and GOLDSTEIN, I. L. (1966), 'Complex monitoring and its relation to the classical problem of vigilance', *Organ. Behav. Hum. Perform.*, vol. 1, pp. 129–50.

HOWLAND, D., and WIENER, E. L. (1963), 'The system monitor', in Buckner, D. N., and McGrath, J. J. (eds.), *Vigilance: A Symposium*, McGraw-Hill, pp. 217–23.

HUMPHRIES, M., and MCINTYRE, J. (1963a), 'Effect of interpolated monocular and binocular visual reaction time activity on reminiscence in pursuit rotor performance', *Percept. mot. Skills*, vol. 17, pp. 333–4.

HUMPHRIES, M., and MCINTYRE, J. (1963b), 'An attempt to find a locus of temporary work decrement in pursuit rotor performance', *Percept. mot. Skills*, vol. 17, pp. 397–8.

JENKINS, H. M. (1958), 'The effect of signal rate on performance in visual monitoring', *Amer. J. Psychol.*, vol. 71, pp. 647–61.

JERISON, H. J. (1963), 'On the decrement function in human vigilance', in Buckner, D. N., and McGrath, J. J. (eds.), *Vigilance: A Symposium*, McGraw-Hill, pp. 199–212.

JERISON, H. J. (1966), 'Remarks on Colquhoun's "The effect of 'unwanted' signals on performance in a vigilance task"', *Ergonomics*, vol. 9, pp. 413–16.

JERISON, H. J. (1967a), 'Vigilance, discrimination and attention', in Mostofsky, D. I. (ed.), *Attention: A Behavioral Analysis*, Appleton-Century-Crofts.

JERISON, H. J. (1967b), 'Signal detection theory in the analysis of human vigilance', *Human Factors*, vol. 9, pp. 285–8.

JERISON, H. J. (1967c), 'Activation and long-term performance', in Sanders, A. F. (ed.), *Attention and Performance*, *Acta Psychologica*, vol. 27, pp. 373–89, North-Holland Publishing Co.

JERISON, H. J., and PICKETT, R. M. (1963), 'Vigilance: a review and re-evaluation', *Human Factors*, vol. 5, pp. 211–38.

JERISON, H. J., and PICKETT, R. M. (1964), 'Vigilance: the importance of the elicited observing rate', *Science*, vol. 143, pp. 970–71.

JERISON, H. J., PICKETT, R. M., and STENSON, H. H. (1965), 'The elicited observing rate and decision processes in vigilance', *Human Factors*, vol. 7, pp. 107–28.

JERISON, H. J., and WING, J. F. (1961), 'Human vigilance and operant behavior', *Science*, vol. 133, pp. 880–81.

JERISON, H. J., and WING, J. F. (1963), 'Human vigilance and operant behavior', in Buckner, D. N., and McGrath, J. J. (eds.), *Vigilance: A Symposium*, McGraw-Hill, pp. 34–8.

JOHNSON, E. M., and PAYNE, M. C., Jr. (1966), 'Vigilance: effects of frequency of knowledge of results', *J. appl. Psychol.*, vol. 50, pp. 33–4.

JOHNSTON, W. A., HOWELL, W. C., and GOLDSTEIN, I. L. (1966), 'Human vigilance as a function of signal frequency and stimulus density', *J. exp. Psychol.*, vol. 72, pp. 736–43.

KAMIYA, J. (1969), 'Operant control of the EEG alpha rhythm and some of its reported effects on consciousness', in Tart, C. S. (ed.), *Altered States of Consciousness*, Wiley, pp. 507–18.

KAPPAUF, W. E., and POWE, W. E. (1959), 'Performance decrement on an audio-visual checking task', *J. exp. Psychol.*, vol. 57, pp. 49–56.

KERSTIN, S., and EYSENCK, H. J. (1965), 'Pursuit rotor performance as a function of different degrees of distraction', *Life Sciences*, vol. 4, pp. 889–97.

KIDD, J. S., and MICOCCI, A. (1964), 'Maintenance of vigilance in an auditory monitoring task', *J. appl. Psychol.*, vol. 48, pp. 13–15.

KIRK, N. S. (1962), *Visual Thresholds and Vigilance*, Thesis.

KIRK, R. E., and HECHT, E. (1963), 'Maintenance of vigilance by programmed noise', *Percept. mot. Skills*, vol. 16, pp. 553–60.

KLEMMER, E. T. (1956), 'Time uncertainty in simple reaction time', *J. exp. Psychol.*, vol. 51, pp. 179–84.

KULP, R. A., and ALLUISI, E. A. (1967), 'Effects of stimulus–response uncertainty on watchkeeping performance and choice reactions', *Percept. Psychophys.*, vol. 2, pp. 511–15.

LATIES, V. G., and WEISS, B. (1960), 'Human observing behavior after signal detection', *J. exp. anal. Behav.*, vol. 3, pp. 27–33.

LEVINE, J. M. (1966), 'The effect of values and costs on the detection and identification of signals in auditory vigilance', *Human Factors*, vol. 8, pp. 525–38.

LINDSLEY, D. B. (1960), 'Attention, consciousness, sleep and wakefulness', in Field, J. (ed.), *Handbook of Physiology*, American Physiological Society, section 1, vol. 3, pp. 1553–94.

LOEB, M., and BINFORD, J. R. (1963), 'Some factors influencing the effective auditory intensive difference limen', *J. Acoust. Soc. Amer.*, vol. 35, pp. 884–91.

LOEB, M., and BINFORD, J. R. (1964), 'Vigilance for auditory intensity change as a function of preliminary feedback and confidence level', *Human Factors*, vol. 6, pp. 445–58.

LOEB, M., and BINFORD, J. R. (1968), 'Variation in performance on auditory and visual monitoring tasks as a function of signal and stimulus frequencies', *Percept. Psychophys.*, vol. 4, pp. 361–6.

LOEB, M., and HAWKES, G. R. (1961), 'The effect of rise and decay time on vigilance for weak auditory and cutaneous stimuli', *Percep. mot. Skills*, vol. 13, pp. 235–42.

LOEB, M., and HAWKES, G. R. (1962), 'Detection of differences in duration of acoustic and electrical cutaneous stimuli in vigilance tasks', *J. Psychol.*, vol. 54, pp. 101–11.

LOEB, M., and SCHMIDT, E. A. (1963), 'A comparison of the effects of different kinds of information in maintaining efficiency on an auditory vigilance task', *Ergonomics*, vol. 6, pp. 75–81.

LUCE, T. S. (1964), 'Vigilance as a function of stimulus variety and response complexity', *Human Factors*, vol. 6, pp. 101–10.

MACKWORTH, J. F. (1963a), 'The effect of intermittent signal probability upon vigilance', *Canad. J. Psychol.*, vol. 17, pp. 82–9.

MACKWORTH, J. F. (1963b), 'Effect of reference marks on the detection of signals on a clock-face', *J. appl. Psychol.*, vol. 47, pp. 196–201.

MACKWORTH, J. F. (1963c), 'The relation between the visual image and post-perceptual immediate memory', *J. verb. Learn. verb. Behav.*, vol. 2, pp. 75–85.

MACKWORTH, J. F. (1964), 'The effect of true and false knowledge of results on the detectability of signals in a vigilance task', *Canad. J. Psychol.*, vol. 18, pp. 106–17.

MACKWORTH, J. F. (1965a), 'The effect of amphetamine on the detectability of signals in a vigilance task', *Canad. J. Psychol.*, vol. 19, pp. 104–9.

MACKWORTH, J. F. (1965b), 'Decision interval and signal detectability in a vigilance task', *Canad. J. Psychol.*, vol. 19, pp. 111–17.

MACKWORTH, J. F. (1965c), 'Deterioration of signal detectability during a vigilance task as a function of background event rate', *Psychon. Sci.*, vol. 3, p. 421.

MACKWORTH, J. F. (1966), 'Perceptual coding as a factor in short-term memory', *Canad. J. Psychol.*, vol. 20, pp. 18–33.

MACKWORTH, J. F. (1968a), 'The effect of signal rate on performance in two kinds of vigilance task', *Human Factors*, vol. 10, pp. 11–18.

MACKWORTH, J. F. (1968b), 'Vigilance, arousal and habituation', *Psychol. Rev.*, vol. 75, pp. 308–22.

MACKWORTH, J. F. (1969), *Vigilance and Habituation: A Neuropsychological Approach*, Penguin Books.

MACKWORTH, J. F., and TAYLOR, M. M. (1963), 'The d′ measure of signal detectability in vigilance-like situations', *Canad. J. Psychol.*, vol. 17, pp. 302–25.

MACKWORTH, N. H. (1950), 'Researches in the measurement of human performance', *M.R.C. Spec. Report 268*, H.M.S.O.; reprinted in Sinaiko, H. A. (ed.) (1961), *Selected Papers on Human Factors in the Design and Use of Control Systems*, Dover Publications, pp. 174–331.

MACKWORTH, N. H. (1957), 'Vigilance', *The Advancement of Science*, vol. 53, pp. 389–93.

MACKWORTH, N. H. (1968), 'The wide-angle reflection eye camera for visual choice and pupil size', *Percept. Psychophys.*, vol. 3, pp. 32–4.

MACKWORTH, N. H., KAPLAN, I. T., and METLAY, W. (1964), 'Eye movements during vigilance', *Percept. mot. Skills*, vol. 18, pp. 397–402.

MACKWORTH, N. H., and MACKWORTH, J. F. (1958a), 'Eye fixations recorded on changing visual scenes by the television eye-marker', *J. Opt. Soc.Amer.*, vol. 48, pp. 439 et seq.

MACKWORTH, N. H., and MACKWORTH, J. F. (1958b), 'Visual search for successive decisions', *Brit. J. Psychol.*, vol. 49, pp. 211–21.

MACKWORTH, N. H., and MORANDI, A. J. (1967), 'The gaze selects informative details within pictures', *Percept. Psychophys.*, vol. 2, pp. 547–52.

MACKWORTH, N. H., and OTTO, D. (in press), 'Habituation of the visual orienting response in young children', *Percept. Psychophys.*

MALMO, R. B. (1959), 'Activation: a neuropsychological dimension', *Psych. Rev.*, vol. 66, pp. 367–86.

MARTZ, R. L. (1966), 'Signal presentation rate, auditory threshold and group vigilance', *Percept. mot Skills*, vol. 23, pp. 463–9.

MARTZ, R. L. (1967), 'Auditory vigilance as affected by signal rate and intersignal interval variability', *Percept. mot. Skills*, vol. 24, pp. 195–203.

McCORMACK, P. D. (1958), 'Performance in a vigilance task as a function of interstimulus interval and interpolated rest', *Canad. J. Psychol.*, vol. 12, pp. 242–6.

McCORMACK, P. D. (1959), 'Performance in a vigilance task with and without knowledge of results', *Canad. J. Psychol.*, vol. 13, pp. 68–72.

McCORMACK, P. D. (1967), 'A two-factor theory of vigilance in the light of recent studies', in Sanders, A. F. (ed.), *Attention and Performance*, *Acta Psychologica*, vol. 27, pp. 400-9, North-Holland Publishing Co.

McCORMACK, P. D., and PRYSIAZNIUK, A. W. (1961), 'Reaction time and regularity of inter-stimulus interval', *Percept. mot. Skills*, vol. 13, pp. 15–18.

McCORMACK, P. D., BINDING, F. R. S., and CHYLINSKI, J. (1962), 'Effects on reaction time of knowledge of results of performance', *Percept. mot. Skills*, vol. 14, pp. 367–72.

McCORMACK, P. D., BINDING, F. R. S., and McELHERAN, W. G. (1963), 'Effects on RT of partial knowledge of results of performance', *Percept. mot. Skills*, vol. 17, pp. 279–81.

McCORMACK, P. D., and McELHERAN, W. G. (1963), 'Follow-up of effects on RT with partial knowledge of results', *Percept. mot. Skills*, vol. 17, pp. 565–6.

McCORMACK, P. D., and PRYSIAZNIUK, A. W. (1961), 'Reaction time and regularity of inter-stimulus interval', *Percept. mot. Skills*, vol. 13, pp. 15–18.

McDONALD, R. D., and BURNS, S. B. (1964), 'Visual vigilance and brain damage: an empirical study', *J. Neurol., Neurosurg. Psychiat.*, vol. 27, pp. 206–9.

McFARLAND, R. A., HOLWAY, A. N., and HURVISCH, L. M. (1942), *Studies of Visual Fatigue,* Harvard Graduate School of Business Administration Report., pp. 160 et seq.

McGRATH, J. J. (1960), 'The effect of irrelevant environmental stimulations on vigilance performance', *Technical Report*, no. 6, Human Factors Research, Inc.

McGRATH, J. J. (1963a), 'Irrelevant stimulation and vigilance performance', in Buckner, D. N., and McGrath, J. J. (eds.), *Vigilance: A Symposium*, McGraw-Hill, pp. 3–18.

McGRATH, J. J. (1963b), 'Some problems of definition and criteria in the study of vigilance performance', in Buckner, D. N., and McGrath, J. J. (eds.), *Vigilance: A Symposium*, McGraw-Hill, pp. 227–36.

McGRATH, J. J. (1965), 'Performance sharing in an audio-visual task', *Human Factors*, vol. 7, pp. 141–54.

McGRATH, J. J., and HARABEDIAN, A. (1963), 'Signal detection as a function of intersignal-interval duration', in Buckner, D. N., and McGrath, J. J. (eds.), *Vigilance: A Symposium*, McGraw-Hill, pp. 102–9.

McGRATH, J. J., and O'HANLON, J. (1967), 'Temporal orientation and vigilance performance', in A. F. Sanders (ed.), *Attention and Performance, Acta Psychologica*, vol. 27, pp. 410–19, North-Holland Publishing Co.

MIRABELLA, A., and GOLDSTEIN, D. A. (1967), 'The effects of ambient noise upon signal detection', *Human Factors*, vol. 9, pp. 277–84.

MONTAGUE, W. E., and WEBBER, C. E. (1965), 'Effects of KR and differential monetary reward on six uninterrupted hours of monitoring', *Human Factors*, vol. 7, pp. 173–80.

MONTAGUE, W. E., WEBBER, C. E., and ADAMS, J. A. (1965), 'The effects of signal rate and response complexity on eighteen hours of visual monitoring', *Human Factors*, vol. 7, pp. 163–72.

MONTY, R. A. (1962), 'Effects of post-detection response complexity on subsequent monitoring behavior', *Human Factors*, vol. 4, pp. 201–8.

MORAY, N. (1967), 'Where is capacity limited? A survey and a model', in Sanders, A. F. (ed.), *Attention and Performance, Acta Psychologica*, vol. 27, pp. 84–92, North-Holland Publishing Co.

MOWRER, O. H. (1940), 'Preparatory set (expectancy): some methods of measurement', *Psychol. Monog.*, vol. 52, no. 2, whole no. 233.

NACHMIAS, J. (1968), 'Effects of presentation probability and number of response alternatives on simple visual detection', *Percept. Psychophys.*, vol. 3, pp. 151–5.

OBRIST, W. D. (1965), 'Electroencephalographic approach to age changes in response speed', in Welford, A. T., and Birren, J. E. (eds.), *Behavior, Ageing and the Nervous System*, Thomas.

O'HANLON, J., SCHMIDT, A., and BAKER, C. H. (1965), 'Doppler discrimination and the effect of a visual alertness indicator upon detection of auditory sonar signals in a sonar watch', *Human Factors*, vol. 7, no. 12, pp. 129–40.

OLDS, J., and MILNER, P. (1954), 'Positive reinforcement produced by electrical stimulation of the septal area and other regions of the rat brain', *J. comp. physiol. Psychol.*, vol. 47, pp. 419–27.

PICKENS, R., MEISCH, R., and McGUIRE, L. E. (1967), 'Methamphetamine reinforcement in rats', *Psychon. Sci.*, vol. 8, pp. 371–2.

POLLACK, I., and KNAFF, P. R. (1958), 'Maintenance of alertness by a loud auditory signal', *J. Acoust. Soc. Amer.*, vol. 30, pp. 1013–16.

POULTON, E. C. (1960), 'The optimal perceptual load in a paced auditory inspection task', *Brit. J. Psychol.*, vol. 51, pp. 127–39.

POULTON, E. C. (1966), 'Engineering psychology', *Ann. Rev. Psychol.*, vol. 17, pp. 177–200.

ROSENQUIST, H. S. (1965), 'The visual response component of rotary pursuit tracking', *Percept. mot. Skills*, vol. 21, pp. 555–60.

SANDERS, A. F. (ed.) (1967), *Attention and Performance*, North-Holland Publishing Co.; reprinted as a book from *Acta Psychologica*, vol. 27.

SIPOWICZ, R. R., WARE, J. R., and BAKER, R. A. (1962), 'The effect of reward and knowledge of results on the performance of a simple vigilance task', *J. exp. Psychol.*, vol. 64, pp. 58–61.

SKINNER, B. F. (1938), *The Behavior of Organisms*, Appleton-Century-Crofts.

SMITH, R. L., LUCACCINI, L. F., GROTH, H., and LYMAN, J. (1966), 'Effects of anticipatory alerting signals and a compatible secondary task on vigilance performance', *J. appl. Psychol.*, vol. 50, pp. 240–46.

SMITH, R. P., WARM, J. S., and ALLUISI, E. A. (1966), 'Effects of temporal uncertainty on watchkeeping performance', *Percept. Psychophys.*, vol. 1, pp. 293–329.

SOKOLOV, E. N. (1963), *Perception and the Conditioned Reflex*, Pergamon Press.

SPILKER, B., KAMIYA, J., CALLEWAY, E., and YEAGER, C. L. (1969), 'Visual evoked responses in subjects trained to control alpha rhythms', *Psychophys.*, vol. 5, pp. 683–95.

SPONG, P., HAIDER, M., and LINDSLEY, D. B. (1965), 'Selective attentiveness and evoked cortical responses to visual and auditory stimuli', *Science*, vol. 148, pp. 395–7.

STERN, R. M. (1966), 'Performance and physiological arousal during two vigilance tasks varying in signal presentation rate', *Percept. mot. Skills*, vol. 23, pp. 691–700.

SUBOSKI, M. D. (1966), 'Bisensory signal detection', *Psychon. Sci.*, vol. 6, pp. 57–8.

SWETS, J. A. (1964), *Signal Detection and Recognition by Human Observers*, Wiley.

TAIMNI, I. K. (1965), *The Science of Yoga*, Theosophical Publishing House.

TAYLOR, M. M. (1965), 'Detectability measures in vigilance: comment on a paper by Wiener, Poock, and Steele', *Percept. mot. Skills*, vol. 20, pp. 1217–21.

TAYLOR, M. M. (1966), 'The effect of the square root of time on continuing perceptual tasks', *Percept. Psychophys.*, vol. 1, pp. 113–19.

TAYLOR, M. M. (1967), 'Detectability theory and the interpretation of vigilance data', in Sanders, A. F. (ed.), *Attention and Performance*, *Acta Psychologica*, vol. 27, pp. 390–99, North-Holland Publishing Co.

TAYLOR, M. M., LINDSAY, P. H., and FORBES, S. M. (1967), 'Quantification of shared capacity processing in auditory and visual discrimination', in Sanders, A. F. (ed.), *Attention and Performance*, *Acta Psychologica*, vol. 27, pp. 223–9, North-Holland Publishing Co.

TEICHNER, W. H. (1962), 'Probability of detection and speed of response in simple monitoring', *Human Factors*, vol. 4, pp. 181–6.

THOMPSON, L. W., OPTON, E., Jr, and COHEN, L. D. (1963), 'Effects of age, presentation speed and sensory modality on performance of a "vigilance" task', *J. Geront.*, vol. 18, pp. 366–9.

TRABASSO, T., and BOWER, G. H. (1968), *Attention in Learning Theory and Research*, Wiley.

TREISMAN, A. (1960), 'Contextual cues in selective listening', *Quart. J. exp. Psychol.*, vol. 12, pp. 242–8.

TREISMAN, M. (1964), 'Noise and Weber's Law: the discrimination of brightness and other dimensions', *Psychol. Rev.*, vol. 71, pp. 314–30.

TREISMAN, M. (1966), 'A statistical decision model for sensory discrimination which predicts Weber's Law and other sensory laws: some results of a computer simulation', *Percept. Psychophys.*, vol. 1, pp. 203–30.

TULVING, E., and LINDSAY, P. H. (1967), 'Identification of simultaneously presented simple visual and auditory stimuli', in Sanders, A. F. (ed.), *Attention and Performance*, *Acta Psychologica*, vol. 27, pp. 101–9, North-Holland Publishing Co.

WALLIS, D., and SAMUEL, J. A. (1961), 'Some experimental studies of radar operating', *Ergonomics*, vol. 4, pp. 155–68.

WALTER, W. G. (1964a), 'The convergence and interaction of visual, auditory and tactile responses in human non-specific cortex', in Whipple, N. R. (ed.), *Sensory Evoked Response in Man*, New York Academy of Sciences, *Ann. N.Y. Acad. Sciences*, vol. 112, pp. 320–61.

WALTER, W. G. (1964b), 'Slow potential waves in the human brain associated with expectancy, attention and decision', *Arch. Psych. Zeitschrift f.d. ges. Neurologie*, vol. 206, pp. 309–22.

WALTER, W. G., COOPER, R., ALDRIDGE, V. J., McCALLUM, W. C., and WINTER, A. L. (1964), 'Contingent negative variation: an electric sign of sensorimotor association and expectancy in the human brain', *Nature*, vol. 203, pp. 380–84.

WARE, J. R. (1961), 'Effects of intelligence on signal detection in visual and auditory monitoring,' *Percept. mot. Skills*, vol. 13, pp. 99–102.

WARE, J. R., and BAKER, R. A. (1964), 'Effects of method of presentation, modes and response category knowledge of results on detection performance in a vigilance task', *J. engin. Psychol.*, vol. 3, pp. 111–16.

WARE, J. R., BAKER, R. A., and DRUCKER, E. (1964), 'Sustained vigilance. II. Signal detection for two-man teams during a twenty-four-hour watch', *J. engin. Psychol.*, vol. 3, pp. 104–10.

WARE, J. R., BAKER, R. A., and SHELDON, R. W. (1964), 'Effect of increasing signal load on detection performance in a vigilance task', *Percept. mot. Skills*, vol. 18, pp. 105–6.

WARE, J. R., KOWAL, B., and BAKER, R. A. (1964), 'The role of experiment attitude and contingent reinforcement in a vigilance task', *Human Factors*, vol. 6, pp. 111–15.

WARE, J. R., SIPOWICZ, R. R., and BAKER, R. A. (1961), 'Auditory vigilance in repeated sessions', *Percept. mot. Skills*, vol. 13, pp. 127–9.

WASAK, M., and OBRIST, W. D. (1969), 'Relationship of slow potential changes to response speed and motivation in man', *Electroenceph. clin. Neurophys.*, vol. 27, pp. 113–120.

WEBB, W. B., and WHERRY, R. J. (1960), 'Vigilance in prolonged and repeated sessions', *Percept. mot. Skills*, vol. 10, pp. 111–13.

WEBBER, C. E., and ADAMS, J. A. (1964), 'Effects of visual display mode on six hours of visual monitoring', *Human Factors*, vol. 6, pp. 13–20.

WEIDENFELLER, E. W., BAKER, R. A., and WARE, J. R. (1962), 'Effects of knowledge of results (true and false) on vigilance performance', *Percept. mot. Skills*, vol. 14, pp. 211–15.

WEINER, H., and ROSS, S. (1962), 'The effects of "unwanted" signals and d-amphetamine sulfate on observer responses', *J. appl. Psychol.*, vol. 46, pp. 135–41.

WIENER, E. L. (1963), 'Knowledge of results and signal rate in monitoring', *J. appl. Psychol.*, vol. 47, pp. 214–21.

WIENER, E. L. (1964a), 'Transfer of training in monitoring: signal amplitude', *Percept. mot. Skills*, vol. 18, p. 104.

WIENER, E. L. (1964b), 'Multiple channel monitoring', *Ergonomics*, vol. 7, pp. 453–60.

WIENER, E. L. (1967), 'Transfer of training from one monitoring task to another', *Ergonomics*, vol. 10, pp. 649–58.

WIENER, E. L. (1968), 'Training for vigilance: repeated sessions with knowledge of results', *Ergonomics*, vol. 11, pp. 547–56.

WIENER, E. L., and ATTWOOD, D. A. (1968), 'Training for vigilance: combined cueing and knowledge of results', *J. appl. Psychol.*, vol. 52, pp. 474–9.

WIENER, E. L., POOCK, G. K., and STEELE, M. (1964), 'Effect of time-sharing on monitoring performance: simple arithmetic as a loading task', *Percept. mot. Skills*, vol. 19, pp. 435–40.

WILKINSON, R. T. (1959), 'Rest pauses in a task affected by lack of sleep', *Ergonomics*, vol. 2, pp. 373–80.

WILKINSON, R. T. (1960), 'The effect of lack of sleep on visual watchkeeping', *Quart. J. exp. Psychol.*, vol. 7, pp. 36–40.

WILKINSON, R. T. (1961a), 'Interaction of lack of sleep with knowledge of results, repeated testing and individual differences', *J. exp. Psychol.*, vol. 62, pp. 263–71.

WILKINSON, R. T. (1961b), 'Comparison of paced, unpaced, irregular and continuous display in watchkeeping', *Ergonomics*, vol. 4, pp. 259–67.

WILKINSON, R. T. (1962), 'Muscle tension during mental work under sleep deprivation', *J. exp. Psychol.*, vol. 64, pp. 565–71.

WILKINSON, R. T. (1963), 'Interaction of noise with knowledge of results and sleep deprivation', *J. exp. Psychol.*, vol. 66, pp. 332–7.

WILKINSON, R. T. (1964), 'Artificial "signals" as an aid to an inspection task', *Ergonomics*, vol. 7, pp. 63–72.

WILKINSON, R. T., MORLOCK, H. C., and WILLIAMS, H. L. (1966), 'Evoked cortical response during vigilance', *Psychon. Sci.*, vol. 4, pp. 221–2.

ZUERCHER, J. D. (1965), 'The effects of extraneous stimulation on vigilance', *Human Factors*, vol. 7, pp. 101–6.

ZWISLOCKI, J., MAIRE, F., FELDMAN, A. S., and RUBIN, H. (1958), 'On the effect of practice and motivation on the threshold of audibility', *J. Acoust. Soc. Amer.*, vol. 30, pp. 254–62.

Acknowledgements

The author is grateful for the financial and psychological support of the Radcliffe Institute, Cambridge, Massachusetts, and also for the advice and support of Professor Pribram.

Thanks are due to the authors of each figure for their permission to reproduce. Full source details will be found in the reference list. Thanks are due to the following publishers for permission to reproduce copyright material:

Figures 13, 14, 20   American Psychological Association, copyright 1964, 1966, 1967

Figures 3a, 3b, 16   *Canadian Journal of Psychology*, Canadian Psychological Association

Figure 18   Elias Press Ltd

Figures 8a, 8b, 8c, 9   Johns Hopkins Press Ltd

Figure 10   North-Holland Publishing Co.

Figures 6, 15   Psychonomic Journals Inc.

Figures 3a, 3b, 12, 17, 17a   *Perceptual and Motor Skills*, Southern Universities Press

Figure 7   *Ergonomics*, Taylor & Francis

Figure 11   University of Illinois Press

Figure 1   John Wiley & Sons

Index